Stadium Stories:

Notre Dame Fighting Irish

Colorful Tales of the Blue and Gold

Eric Hansen

The Globe Pequot Press

GUILFORD, CONNECTICUT

Stadium Stories is a trademark of Morris Book Publishing, LLC.

Text design: Casey Shain
Cover photos : Joe Raymond (top left, top right, middle left, bottom left, bottom right) and *South Bend Tribune* (middle right).

Library of Congress Cataloging-in-Publication Data
Hansen, Eric C. (Eric Christian), 1960–
    Stadium stories : Notre Dame Fighting Irish : colorful tales of the blue and gold / Eric C. Hansen.
        p. cm. – (Stadium stories series)
    ISBN 0-7627-3139-7
    1. Notre Dame Fighting Irish (Football team)
2. University of Notre Dame — Football — History. I. Title: Notre Dame Fighting Irish. II. Title. III. Series.

GV958.U54H36 2004
796.332'63'0977289–dc22   2004052397

Manufactured in the United States of America
First Edition/First Printing

Contents

To Antonio and Blake;
my sons and my inspiration

Everyday Heroes

The Walk-on Tradition

Before there was *Rudy*, there was Michael Oriard, whose Notre Dame experience was never made into a movie but easily could have been. How many other aspiring college football players walk into their dermatologist's office for help with their complexion and walk away with a road map to a dream?

That's how it all started for Oriard, a tough, spindly kid from Spokane, Washington, who was never formally recruited for football by any college—including Notre Dame—but wound up, first, a starter for former Irish coach Ara Parseghian in 1968, then a captain and an All-American the following season before wrapping a brief-but-productive pro football career around graduate school.

"Things really broke for me, and I really had kind of a storybook, fairy-tale existence at Notre Dame, but that's only true of the rough outlines," said the 1970 Notre Dame graduate. "Sure, when I got my first start the fifth game of my junior season, you could almost hear the violins in the background. But my day-to-day experience was full of ups and downs. It was a common experience."

But like so many of Notre Dame's walk-ons, those common experiences have helped lead to extraordinary moments beyond Notre Dame.

Oriard, one of the first and few Irish walk-ons who went on to All-America status, currently serves as an English professor at Oregon State University and has written a number of groundbreaking books, including several dealing with sports. His dogged attitude in the face of long odds, tested and tempered at Notre Dame, helped make many of those book projects possible.

After Rudy the player, but before *Rudy* the movie, there was Reggie Ho, the diminutive walk-on kicker who helped make Notre Dame's last national championship season (1988) possible. He has taken the resilience and mind-calming skills he learned as a member of the Irish football team and has applied them to his practice as a cardiologist at Thomas Jefferson Medical Center in Philadelphia.

More recently, there was Joe Recendez, who played just 1:48 during his Notre Dame football career. But every one of those 108 seconds came during the 2000 season—just months after undergoing surgery for testicular cancer. Three and a half years later, he graduated from law school at the University of Illinois, eager to put his second chance at life into a context where he could make a difference for others.

Even Notre Dame's current football coach, Tyrone Willingham, was a walk-on—albeit for Michigan State. Willingham grew up with the same passion for Notre Dame as did most of the Irish walk-ons over the years. But Notre Dame wasn't interested in the 5' 6", 135-pound quarter-back/center fielder, as was the case with ninety-seven of the other ninety-nine schools Willingham wrote to during his senior year in high school at Jacksonville, North Carolina. Had Notre Dame relented or had Willingham pushed the issue harder, his college career might have overlapped that of Notre Dame's most famous walk-on, Daniel "Rudy" Ruettiger.

Unfairly and inaccurately, almost every Notre Dame walk-on story told these days includes some reference to

Rudy—the person, the movie, or both. Columbia/Tristar released the 112-minute story of Ruettiger in 1993, the details of which are ingrained in most Notre Dame fans' consciousness: A young boy who was told he wasn't good enough, smart enough, or talented enough to chase his dream of attending Notre Dame, initially buys into what he thought would be his drab destiny. After Ruettiger graduated from high school, the script has him following his brothers and father into the steel mills, but a death of a close friend (in real life, it was the death of two close friends) shook Ruettiger out of his sleepwalk through life and onto a path that would eventually land him at Notre Dame.

There would be more hurdles at Notre Dame. Rudy was initially treated as little more than a tackling dummy. His resilience, however, eventually earned the respect of his teammates and coaches. And in Rudy's final opportunity to play, he not only gets in during the final twenty-seven seconds against Georgia Tech, but makes the last tackle in a 24–3 Irish triumph, the final home game of the 1975 season. Coincidentally, the player who Rudy tackled was Georgia Tech quarterback *Rudy* Allen.

"It's not a Notre Dame story or a football story," said Ruettiger, who has parlayed the film into a successful public speaking career for himself. "It's a story about life—the dream, the struggle, and the victory of it. It didn't have a complicated message or try to change the world. It's just a common little movie that had a big impact on America."

Getting the movie made, however, was almost as much of a struggle as any of the events portrayed in the movie.

Ruettiger's initial exploits garnered a fifteen-paragraph write-up in the local *South Bend Tribune*—roughly a paragraph for every two seconds of action Ruettiger saw. In the

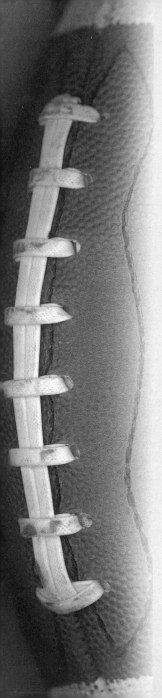

Life after *Rudy*

The 1993 release of the movie *Rudy* elevated Notre Dame graduate Daniel E. Ruettiger to the status of world's most noted football walk-on.

Life after *Rudy* has been good for both Ruettiger and Notre Dame's walk-ons, who seem to slip into the spotlight a little more regularly since the film came out. Ruettiger has since married and moved to Henderson, Nevada, near Las Vegas. "With my public speaking career taking off, it was the easiest place to fly in and out of," he said.

He has two small children, daughter Jessica and son Danny. "It's a whole new life," he said. "It gives you a new perspective on life."

And Rudy gave the nation a new perspective—if not appreciation—for walk-on football players. However, it didn't create a stampede to South Bend.

The same constraints that had always limited Notre Dame's walk-ons remain in place now. Those that aren't snagged by the school's high academic standards are sometimes eliminated by the economic reality of paying one's own way to Notre Dame.

But Notre Dame still seems to attract quality. Four walk-ons played prominent roles for the 2003 team: kicker/punter D. J. Fitzpatrick, holder Matt Krueger, long snapper Casey Dunn, and fullback Josh Schmidt. The season before, walk-on Pat

Dillingham appeared in seven games at quarterback for the Irish, winning his only start.

Sometimes Notre Dame's best walk-ons are walk-offs from other sports. All-America cornerback Shane Walton, who graduated in the spring of 2003, was one of the best players on the Irish men's soccer team prior to trying football.

Former coach Bob Davie initially thought Walton was coming out as a kicker. Notre Dame had some kicking woes during the Davie era, and another soccer standout was open to the idea of helping out.

Jen Grubb, an All-American for the Notre Dame women's soccer team, had been a kicker at Conant High School in Hoffman Estates, Illinois, and became the first female ever to score a point in an Illinois high school football game. Her longest field goal in a game in high school was 37 yards, while her longest in practice was 51.

"If they want me, they know where to find me," Grubb said in the fall of 1998.

Another Davie era walk-on was notable because of the number he wore: 45. Matt Sarb, a defensive back, wore the number in honor of Rudy. Matt's father, Pat, was a scholarship defensive back in the mid-1970s and was one of three players who volunteered to give up his jersey so that Rudy could play in the final home game of his senior season.

Notre Dame's current coach, Tyrone Willingham, has a special spot in his heart for walk-ons, because he was one himself—at Michigan State. "When you're a walk-on, you have a different appreciation for athletics," Willingham said. "I think you value athletics, not because you have a scholarship, but because you love the sport and the competition.

"It's definitely different than other athletes. You don't have to have a crowd to enjoy playing. I think it has given me the perspective that, as an underdog, you can overcome. I believe that whether you're smaller in stature or you weren't ranked in some category that you can accomplish and be successful.

"Hopefully, that has transcended my playing days and worked into my coaching."

article, sportswriter Bill Moor refers to Ruettiger as "Ruetty" rather than Rudy.

> "Can you imagine lining up across from Ross Browner or Willie Fry all day and suddenly you see Ruetty across from you?" then–Notre Dame defensive line coach Joe Yonto told Moor. "He finessed his man on the giggle." But Yonto was quick to add, "This is great for team morale."

Yet Ruettiger quickly faded into the blur of head coach Dan Devine's first season. Moor did have recollections of Rudy, perhaps largely because he was brave/foolish enough to step into the boxing ring with him for an exhibition match. But most of the Rudy tales were told by Ruettiger himself.

"People would become engaged by the story and they'd tell me, 'You ought to make that into a movie,' " he recalled. "But how do you make a movie? I guess you tell the story to the right person, but it's still a lot of work."

The "right person" ended up being a man named John Stratigos, who in turn told his brother, Don, who in turn talked to screenwriter Angelo Pizzo.

"I got introduced to Angelo Pizzo, but it was eight more years before the movie got made," Ruettiger said. "When I flew out to California to meet Angelo, he either forgot I was coming or maybe didn't want to meet me."

Eventually the movie did get made, compressing Ruettiger's life story into a space of less than two hours. Some events were slightly embellished. Groups of important people were squeezed into singular composite characters. Some significant milestones received cursory glances or were cut out altogether.

Some of the more intriguing footnotes in the life of the real Rudy include that he was twenty-seven years old when he made that tackle against Georgia Tech, that he was a live-in security guard in Notre Dame's basketball/hockey facility, that he was actually an all-conference guard at Joliet (Illinois) Catholic Academy, that he originally attended Rockport College on a baseball/wrestling scholarship, that he worked as a turbine operator for Commonwealth Edison, and that he spent two years in the Navy before enrolling first at Holy Cross Junior College in South Bend, then Notre Dame.

He was also a standout boxer in college, finishing runner-up in the campus boxing competition known as the Bengal Bouts one year and winning the light heavyweight division the next year.

"We originally had the boxing in the script," Ruettiger said, "but it had to get cut, so the movie wouldn't be too long. My time in the Navy never got close to making it in, but it was a very important part of my life. It really set me straight. There were a lot of people in the Navy who inspired me."

And now Ruettiger makes it his life's work to inspire others.

One of his own sources of inspiration at Notre Dame was a scholarship quarterback who struggled mightily during the 1974 season. This particular QB was ticketed for the Irish junior varsity team that year, during which three other signal callers (Gary Forystek, Kerry Moriarity, and Mike Falash) attempted more passes than he did. In fact, Joe Montana completed as many passes that year (one in six attempts) to the opposing team as he did to his own. He did, however, punt ten times for a respectable

36.5-yard average. Montana then went on to become a master of comeback victories at Notre Dame before evolving into one of the all-time great QBs in pro football history.

"It was the struggle and his will to overcome it that was inspirational," Ruettiger said of Montana. "That's what hits home with people. When I first started doing public speaking, I didn't get that. I was scared. I thought they wanted to know all about Notre Dame's football history and all that. It finally dawned on me that they just wanted to know what made me tick, man."

Whatever it is, it ticked inside Oriard, too, but in a much different way.

To this day, he cannot place what got him interested in Notre Dame. His mother said he enjoyed watching the film *Knute Rockne, All American* as a child, and Oriard did attend Catholic grade school in Spokane, but during much of Oriard's childhood and adolescent years, Notre Dame football was in a down cycle. He visited several schools on his own, including Idaho and Oregon State. He expressed some interest in heading off to one of the service academies as well, but no one seemed really anxious to reciprocate the interest.

"Recruiting, when I looked back on it, seemed so informal and casual in those days," Oriard said. "I don't know how they ever ended up with the right guys."

Oriard ended up in the right place after making small talk one day with his dermatologist, who happened to be a Notre Dame grad. Dr. James Rotchford then wrote to his alma mater on behalf of Oriard. Word came back that the 6'4", 200-pound lineman would be invited to walk on since there were no scholarships left.

Eventually, Oriard did earn a scholarship for the last three semesters of school, but only after asking his coach, Parseghian, for it. "Maybe I should have asked sooner," Oriard said with a laugh.

It's not likely he would have had the confidence. Prior to starting his first game midway through his junior season, Oriard was shocked at his steady movement up the depth chart.

"I had worked my way up to number two," he said. "But the Monday after the fourth game, there I was, number one. I thought, 'Holy cow.' I couldn't talk to anybody about it. I thought if I did, they'd realize it was a mistake. But it wasn't a mistake. When Saturday finally rolled around, it was a tremendous feeling, but more of a private experience. Nobody carried me off their shoulders like they did in *Rudy*."

At 125 pounds, Reggie Ho was just the right size to carry off the field, however. The 5'5" Hawaii product enrolled at Notre Dame in the last year of the Gerry Faust era with no inkling of playing football.

"Even though I didn't know what I wanted to do with my life, I knew I wanted to focus on academics that first year," Ho said. "I had thoughts of architecture and medicine. And when I made it through my first year with all A's and just one A minus, my thoughts started to drift toward football. I figured there must be more to life than studying."

Had Ho's older brother, Mark, not gone out for the football team at St. Louis High School in Kaneohe, Hawaii, Reggie Ho might never have tried the sport. "I just saw him doing it, and it seemed natural to follow in his footsteps," Ho said.

Earning a spot on the Irish roster wasn't so easy, though. Lou Holtz, who had taken over for Faust, had an open mind

for the little guy. Eventually Ho saw his first action late in his junior season, kicking an extra point in a blowout victory over Navy on Halloween of 1987. The next year, Ho won the kicking job for extra points and short field goals.

He is best remembered for kicking four field goals in a 19–17 victory over Michigan to open the 1988 season, a season that would culminate in a national championship.

Ho's heroics spawned a three-page spread in *Sports Illustrated*, of which Ho was a central figure. But to this day, the humble Ho hasn't read a word of it.

"Was it good?" he said politely.

As good as Ho was, who literally saved Notre Dame's season. He turned down a fifth year of eligibility to embark on medical school. Now, as a cardiologist, he saves lives.

"My Notre Dame experience changed my life," Ho said. "It's not just the victories, it's the perspective on life you receive there. For example, the first thing we did after winning the national championship was to have Mass — before we celebrated, before we met with our friends and family. Lou Holtz himself delivered the homily. That showed all of us there are more important things in life."

No one had to tell that to Joe Recendez, a reserve tight end who had worked his way up to third team by the end of spring practice in 2000. Like Ho, Recendez came to Notre Dame with no intentions of playing football. His father, Joe Sr., had sold the family's home to help finance his only son's education.

Walk-on kicker Reggie Ho (center) celebrates with his teammates after kicking the game-winning field goal against Michigan, September 10, 1988, in South Bend. (Courtesy Joe Raymond)

But Recendez couldn't stay away from football. He played interhall football as a sophomore and walked on to the Irish team as a junior. He was a rarity as a walk-on, coming back for a fifth year. Head coach Bob Davie made it easier by awarding Recendez a scholarship.

But less than a month after ascending to a spot on the depth chart that commanded respect and churned up Recendez's wildest dreams, he learned that he had a cancerous tumor. Recendez wanted to ignore the little stabbing pains as he jogged that spring, but he eventually gave in and saw the doctor. Surgery was first, then radiation treatments, then 15 pounds of weight loss that turned the already undersized tight end into a wide receiver-esque 205 pounds. Then came seemingly endless nausea, a residual effect of the radiation as well as Recendez's ongoing medication regimen.

"My digestive system never really got back to normal that season," he said. "I either threw up after every meal or felt like I was going to. It wasn't until the Fiesta Bowl in Phoenix (January 1, 2001) that I was finally able to eat without the fear of throwing up afterward. And it wasn't until midway through my first year in law school when I could wake up and not have to think about whether I felt 100 percent."

In the summer of 2003, the doctors cleared Recendez for good, assuring him that the cancer wouldn't return. He celebrated by joining a flag football team at the University of Illinois, where he was attending law school.

"It's not the same as Notre Dame," he said of the flag football experience. "But when you've been through what I've been through, you don't take anything for granted."

Joe Recendez, who normally wore Number 13, loosens up at this November 1, 2000 practice. He wore Number 80 in practice on this day because he was practicing with the scout team. *(Courtesy Joe Raymond)*

That includes his alma mater's football team, which he keeps a close eye on—especially the walk-ons. And he ponders how he might make a difference in the lives of others with his law degree.

"People have told me my life story would make a good movie," he said. "Too bad Rudy beat me to it."

This Too Shall Pass

Forward Thinking

T here wasn't really anything that distinguished the trio as they jostled in their seats and counted the hours on the 718-mile-long train trip to West Point, New York. To save money, then–Notre Dame football coach Jesse Harper had brought only eighteen players with him, so it was hardly an imposing group.

Star quarterback Gus Dorais probably looked more like a young porter than a budding legend. The 5'7", 145-pounder from Chippewa Falls, Wisconsin, had a brashness about him, though. So did his friend and sidekick, Knute Rockne, an end for the Irish back in 1913.

At 5'8", 165 pounds, Rockne was small in stature, too — even by that era's standards. But no one dreamed bigger.

Harper dreamed too, but he was more of a pragmatist. Maybe it was the only way to survive. In addition to being Notre Dame's first full-time football coach that year, he was the Irish basketball coach, track coach, and baseball coach, and he was the school's first official athletic director.

For Harper, pondering new frontiers, both on the mental and physical planes, was acceptable, but only if every detail, every decimal point, every decision was calculated, thought through, and measured. So this trip to the East to play powerful Army was a rare whim for the professorial-looking Harper.

Maybe the three of them really could envision the stunning outcome as the train rumbled along the tracks, that Notre Dame would pull one of the great upsets of the time against the overconfident Cadets, even though there was little history to measure it against or national polls with which to quantify it.

What none of them could foresee was how it would change college football and Notre Dame's direction and football lore forever.

"Initially, I was just happy we were going to come out $83 ahead on the deal," a laughing Harper told the *South Bend Tribune*'s Joe Doyle three decades after the fact.

It wasn't just the convincing final score, 35–13, it was the way Notre Dame shocked Army. It was the national stage on which the Irish did it. And it was the fact that first Harper, then Rockne in his coaching days years later, made sure the Fighting Irish program built on the moment rather than letting it rot away as an obscure historical footnote.

Notre Dame threw the football against Army on November 1, 1913, threw it cleverly, threw it often, and totally confounded Notre Dame's heavily favored hosts.

Army had scouted an earlier Irish 62–0 rout of Alma and expected a power running game from Notre Dame. The Cadets did get it, in occasional blasts from Notre Dame fullback Ray Eichenlaub, who at 210 pounds was heftier than any of his linemen. But by then, the Army defense was so bewildered, it couldn't even stop what it had expected in the first place.

After a wobbly start, in which Dorais fumbled on Notre Dame's own 27 yard line and misfired on his first two aerials, the Irish QB heated up to finish 14-of-17 for 243 yards and two touchdowns — unheard of passing numbers in the days when most games were won with brute strength and line plunges.

Rockne was on the receiving end of most of those Dorais strikes, including one of the touchdowns. They certainly didn't invent the pass that day, but they came close to perfecting it and introduced it as a viable option for moving the football rather than the gimmick or desperation play the forward pass had been perceived as being up to that point in football history.

"The press and the football public hailed this new game," said Rockne, whose 40-yard reception from Dorais that day became the longest pass play anywhere on record. "And Notre Dame received credit as the originator of a style of play that we simply systematized."

Rockne and Dorais, though, went to great lengths to systematize it the summer before the 1913 season. The two friends got jobs as lifeguards at a hotel at Cedar Point, a resort and amusement park in northern Ohio on Lake Erie. They were paid room, board, and $12 a week for their labor, but the real payoff came in their idle time. Rockne and Dorais asked Harper if they could borrow a couple of footballs to take with them for the summer.

Legend has it the two spent countless hours on the beach, tossing the football back and forth while curious onlookers shook their heads in disbelief. The reality was that they often ran in the sand to build endurance in their legs, but they worked mostly in seclusion on a grass field trying to figure out how the pass could become a legitimate weapon. The grass field allowed them to perfect timing, to develop pass patterns, and to try different angles and approaches.

Cedar Point and the surrounding city of Sandusky, Ohio, are both apparently quite proud of this thread of Notre Dame history. Both organizations feature the origins

A Passing Fancy

For all the eyes it opened, the minds it bent, and the dreams it stirred, Notre Dame's historic 35–13 upending of Army in 1913 didn't turn Notre Dame into a passing school.

Even Rockne, who was on the receiving end of many of Gus Dorais's ground-breaking aerials that day, only used the pass to open up the run during his unparalleled coaching stint. He never became pass-happy, nor really did any of his successors—even though he helped popularize the forward pass as a player.

"As a coach, Rockne ran the ball probably 60 percent of the time," noted Joe Doyle, *South Bend Tribune* sports editor emeritus and Notre Dame football historian. "Of course, Frank Leahy had some good quarterbacks, but he was still a running coach at heart.

"Ara [Parseghian] was, too, but Ara could use the pass better than anybody else when he

of the Rockne-Dorais connection on their Web sites, although the Sandusky site struggles a bit with historical accuracy. It claims "Rockne and the other Four Horsemen worked at Cedar Point." Rockne actually coached the Four Horsemen a decade later. Then again, Rockne was never the easiest guy to strip the Hollywood embellishment from his true roots.

It is well documented, however, that the passing game had been legalized in 1906, seven years before the Notre Dame–Army clash of 1913. President Theodore Roosevelt, wanted to. He knew how to get guys open. I think if there was one coach who really wanted to throw, it was Hugh Devore [Notre Dame's interim head coach in both 1945 and 1963], but he didn't have the talent to do it."

Only five quarterbacks in Irish history have finished among the top ten passers nationally in a given season: Heisman Trophy winner Angelo Bertelli (1941–1942), Frank Dancewicz (1944), Bob Williams (1950), Ralph Guglielmi (1954), and Rick Mirer (1990–1991).

The Irish haven't been among the top twenty passing teams in the country since 1979, and only once since 1986 has Notre Dame been higher than forty-ninth (thirty-fourth in 1999). Additionally, only sixteen times since 1946 did the Irish offense have a higher statistical rank with its passing game over its running game, and none of those have happened since 1986.

Current Notre Dame head coach Tyrone Willingham, who put up big passing numbers with his teams at Stanford, was expected to come in and do the same at Notre Dame. But he has amended those expectations with a "balanced offense" as his new stated goal.

"I think some of it's tradition and some of it's climate," Doyle said of the lack of infatuation with the passing game at Notre Dame. "You've always played a lot of games in November, and sometimes climate dictates that you run the ball. I don't think it will ever change."

concerned about the brutality of football, first implored the rules committee to make the game safer. John W. Heisman, a longtime coach and football visionary from whom the Heisman Trophy takes its name, also nagged the rules committee to legalize the play. He reportedly first saw a forward pass in an 1895 matchup between Georgia and North Carolina, even though it was not a legal play. The Carolina punter became frantic when the rush came. Fearing he couldn't get the kick off, he threw the ball to a teammate. The referee didn't see the toss and counted the touchdown—the only score of the game—much to Georgia's disdain.

It took a while for the idea to click, though. Flying wedges and mass plays were the order of the day and made football increasingly dangerous. Heisman thought the forward pass could save the game, but he couldn't get Walter Camp, the rules chairman, to agree with him. So Heisman bypassed him and built enough support to get the rule pushed through anyway in 1906.

Still, it was a play that was rarely used. Initially, there was a myriad of restrictions that made the forward pass even less palatable than when Harper and the Irish starting toying with it. For example, a pass that was tipped but not caught was treated as a fumble, a free ball. Moreover, the quarterback had to be 5 yards behind the center before he could throw the pass, making it virtually impossible to catch anyone's defense by surprise.

The ball's shape was another handicap. It was bigger and more awkward than the current model, making it difficult to throw accurately. Most passers tried to fling it rather than throw it, which resulted in wobbly and high throws that allowed defenders to react with ease.

Dorais was credited with being one of the first players to throw spirals. Rockne was supposedly one of the first to catch a pass over his shoulder in stride rather than trapping the ball against the torso. Harper credits himself at different points in his life with inspiring those two evolutions, but he always points to his college coach, Amos Alonzo Stagg, for opening his mind to new possibilities and innovations.

Rockne also became a great admirer of Stagg, who made his name at the University of Chicago. In many

Rockne biographies, it has been written that Rockne, as a coach, invented the backfield shift after watching and admiring the synchronicity of a chorus line. However, in Rockne's own autobiography, he never makes mention of that, but in many of his correspondences he does mention Stagg.

The week after the Army game, when Notre Dame visited Penn State, there would be another passing wrinkle—although this one was quite unintentional. It was the creation of the buttonhook pass play.

Rockne was going out for a pass when he slipped and fell. The Penn State defender kept running, so Rockne was by himself. He picked himself up and caught a pass from Dorais. The two then made it into a planned play—without the falling down part. Rockne would run downfield as fast as he could, stop and turn sharply, while the defender struggled to change his body momentum.

The Irish edged Penn State, 14–7, then went on to defeat Christian Brothers of St. Louis, 20–7, and Texas, 30–7, both on the road, to complete an unbeaten season.

Harper went on to post a 34–5–1 record in five seasons as Notre Dame's football coach, his .863 winning percentage approaching Rockne's (.881) and bettering that of Frank Leahy (.855), the latter regarded in some circles as Notre Dame's best coach ever, given the competition and the challenges he faced. Twenty-five of Harper's thirty-four wins were shutouts.

In five seasons as Notre Dame's basketball coach, Harper was 44–20 (.686), while in baseball he was 63–26 (.708). The Irish basketball team played on an old clay court that had to be rolled and watered daily in those days.

Frank Leahy, pictured here during a 1946 practice session, coached four of Notre Dame's seven Heisman Trophy winners and recruited a fifth in Paul Hornung. (Courtesy South Bend Tribune)

"Basketball was a new game and wasn't highly thought of," said *South Bend Tribune* sports editor emeritus Joe Doyle. "But Jesse [Harper] put his best effort into all the sports he coached.

"He is really highly regarded in coaching circles. The one thing that distinguished him from an innovative standpoint was that he thought football should pay for itself. So he scheduled teams like Nebraska, big-money games, to try to meet that end."

Army's guarantee of $1,000 was not big money, but it was a chance to get Notre Dame on the map. Harper had written to Army in the spring of 1913, hoping to schedule the game.

"You can imagine my surprise and delight when I received a reply from West Point officials," Harper said, "to the effect that they had an open date on November 1, 1913, which we could have."

Because of the tight finances, Harper left assistant Cap Edwards and all but eighteen players and fourteen sets of cleats in South Bend.

"We didn't need eighteen," Harper said with a chuckle. "Eleven men played the entire sixty minutes without taking a timeout."

On the way home, at a stopover at a train station in Buffalo, things continued to go Notre Dame's way. A confused railroad agent mistook the Fighting Irish for Syracuse's football team and shuttled them into a room for breakfast. Moments after Harper and the Notre Dame players finished the feast, Syracuse showed up, fresh off a 43–7 mauling at Michigan, only to find out their meal had been given away.

The aura of the victory—at Army, not at the breakfast table—took on a life of its own and still endures today. *Sports Illustrated* rated the 1913 matchup between Army and Notre Dame as the eleventh greatest game in any sport at any level in the twentieth century.

"There was no paid gate at the game, so the $1,000 guarantee was all we got," Harper said. "There's no telling how much Notre Dame profited from the victory. It spread the school's name throughout the country. And the ultimate return would have to be estimated in the millions. Some say it stands as the most financially significant win in football history."

Of the three central figures who helped make history that day, Rockne was the least likely to ever make it to that point.

His family's decision to immigrate from Voss, Norway, to Chicago was the easy part. Getting the 93 miles from Chicago's Logan Square district to South Bend, Indiana, was the tricky part.

In fact, there were so many capricious events in Rockne's life that should have kept him away from both football and Notre Dame if it weren't for a few fateful twists and an iron clad stubbornness that eventually put Rockne on the eastbound train from South Bend that autumn day in 1913.

The biggest obstacle for Rockne playing football in the first place was his parents' disdain for the game. He was one of the smaller, though faster, players. But he played in a time when size and strength always trumped speed.

One day, when Rockne got pummeled in a sandlot game, his parents refused to allow him to ever play again. They considered football no more than organized mayhem.

But baseball agreed with them. Young Rockne then devoted all his time and passion to that sport until he got into an argument one day. Rockne's crooked nose, which is readily apparent even in photos taken during his coaching days, was a result of that argument that day. He got hit in the face with a bat.

Instead of despair, Rockne reportedly ran home excited. "You think football is a rough game," he told his parents. "Look what I got from baseball."

His parents relented and let Rockne play football in high school, but the 100-pound, 13-year-old stunk at first. What he was good at was track, as a half-miler and a pole vaulter.

He never gave up on football, but he did give up on academics. As bright as he was, Rockne dropped out of school and got a job at the post office. He continued running track in his spare time, for fun, though, rather than what he thought it might lead to.

By Notre Dame's current standards, Rockne never would have had a prayer of admittance. But in that era, Notre Dame opened its doors and arms to ambitious young men who wanted to work their way through school regardless of their academic past.

Still, the 22-year-old would-be freshman figured the University of Illinois would be the best place for him, but two friends and fellow track standouts convinced Rockne it would be easier to get a job in South Bend and that the track team was better.

Rockne, who headed to South Bend with $1,000 and a suitcase, didn't aspire to play football at first. But at Notre Dame, which had only about 400 students at the time, almost every boy played interhall football.

The news of Rockne's prowess found its way to coach Frank Longman, but when Rockne tried out for Longman, it was more like a scene out of *Rudy* than *Knute Rockne, All American*. Longman fashioned Rockne as a fullback, rather than his familiar position, end. And the Norwegian immigrant got humiliated by the older players.

So it was back to track and field for Rockne, who gained confidence while away from football. Dorais, who was the first person Rockne met when he arrived at Notre Dame, stayed in Rockne's corner and helped convince him to come back out as a sophomore.

The second time proved to be a charm, though Rockne almost gave up football and school when his father died. One of his sisters urged him to stay at Notre Dame instead of coming home and trying to support the family financially.

Rockne had his mother's blessing, too, even though she never embraced her son's favorite sport. During Rockne's senior season, two weeks before the seismic Army encounter, he invited her to South Bend for a Notre Dame game against South Dakota.

Rockne had a huge game, and his mother was impressed—with a young man who was doing cartwheels, not her son. The young man was a Fighting Irish cheerleader.

Even after graduation, Rockne's destiny kept being pulled in directions that could have easily derailed his legacy. Rockne's first All-America player as a coach, George Gipp, for example, had to be talked into playing football rather than baseball and was a high-maintenance project on and off the field for his entire Notre Dame career. The Four Horsemen, anonymous and dubbed as freshmen, didn't play their first year either. And Rockne initially wasn't impressed with any of them.

Getting into coaching wasn't easy either. Coaches of the day, including Harper, were not well thought of or well paid (something that changed in the Rockne era of coaching). And as disinterested a student as Rockne was in high school, he appeared headed toward a career in the classroom as an educator.

Rockne worked as a janitor in the chemistry lab during his days as a Notre Dame student and was brilliant at chemistry, so much so that the Reverend Julius Nieuwland, a botany and organic chemistry professor, offered Rockne a graduate assistantship in chemistry. Rockne took it with one stipulation: that he could help Harper coach the football team. Nieuwland could see where Rockne's passion truly lay.

Dorais also went into coaching after World War I. He initially came back to Notre Dame and assisted Rockne with his 1919 squad, Rockne's second overall and his first to go undefeated.

Wrapped around that football season were two basketball and baseball seasons in which Dorais served as head coach, succeeding Harper in both sports. Dorais's two Notre Dame baseball squads went 11–4–1 and 14–6, but his basketball teams were a combined 7–23.

From Notre Dame, Dorais went on to coach Gonzaga's football program, which at the time carried the Fighting Irish nickname rather than its current Bulldogs moniker. Among the stars for Dorais, at a school that considered itself the Notre Dame of the West at the time, was a linebacker named Houston Stockton. His grandson is John Stockton, a former Gonzaga basketball standout and longtime star in the NBA who recently retired.

All in all, Dorais, who also had coaching stops at Loras and the University of Detroit, had a collegiate football record of 150–70–13. He coached the NFL's Detroit Lions from 1943 through 1947 with a modest mark of 20–31–2.

One of Dorais's college losses came at the hands of Rockne and Notre Dame. In 1927, the Irish shut out Detroit in the Motor City, 20–0.

"I think Dorais was a good coach by any standard," the *Tribune*'s Joe Doyle said. "What separated Rockne was that he was a bit of a con artist, a salesman. He knew how to get people on his side and get things done. As a coach, he was more popular and was more dynamic than Gus."

Dorais, however, was more decorated as a player. He was Notre Dame's first consensus All-American and only four-year starter at quarterback for the Irish until 1980, when Blair Kiel came along. (It should be pointed out that freshmen were ineligible to participate in varsity football for a good chunk of the time span between Dorais and Kiel.)

Dorais's real first name was actually Charles, not Gus. He was in a freshman literature course at Notre Dame, and the French illustrator Gustave Doré was brought up in class one day. The names were spelled differently but pronounced the same (dor-RAY), so Dorais's classmates started calling him "Gustave." Later it was shortened to "Gus," and it stuck.

Harper inherited both Rockne and Dorais and coached each one of them only one season. Sadly, both would precede him in death, Rockne in a plane crash in 1931 at age forty-three, Dorais from an illness in 1954 at age sixty-two.

It was Rockne's death that brought Harper back to Notre Dame briefly in the 1930s. Thirty-one days after Rockne's plane nosedived into a field near Bazaar, Kansas,

Harper left his ranch on the other end of the state, in Sitka, to come to Notre Dame to be athletic director.

Harper had walked away from coaching after the 1917 season to go into the cattle ranching business with his wife's family. At Harper's recommendation, Rockne—his top assistant—replaced Harper as head football coach and athletic director, but not without a fight.

"Some of the priests weren't exactly sold on Rock as an assistant football coach, though anyone close to football knew he had an exceptionally sharp mind," Harper said. "Finally, I told one of the objectors, 'If you hire anyone else, you'll be making the biggest mistake Notre Dame ever made.' "

The two men stayed in touch during Rockne's magnificent coaching run (1918–1930). But while Notre Dame football continued its climb to national prominence, Harper's cattle ranch was foundering and was in real trouble in the post–Rockne years during the Depression. Eventually, though, Harper enjoyed a reversal of fortunes when oil was discovered on his property.

Harper was athletic director only from 1931 to 1933 during his second stint at Notre Dame, but he instituted some changes that stayed with Notre Dame for decades. Although Harper was proud of Rockne, he felt his former pupil had lost sight of some important principles. So Harper decreed that any student-athlete must maintain a seventy-seven average (on a one hundred point scale) to remain eligible. He instituted a no-transfer rule to keep Notre Dame from poaching other schools' talented underclassmen, and he organized stricter scholarship guidelines, limiting it to room, board, books, and tuition.

Harper eventually crossed paths again with Dorais. It was after his old quarterback had gotten out of coaching and took over an automobile dealership in Wabash, Indiana.

"I remember him telling me how happy he was," Harper said in 1951, "and what a fool he'd been to take all those headaches."

Harper never missed the stress of coaching, and railed against fans and alumni for being too zealous.

"I certainly wouldn't advise a young fellow to go in for coaching," Harper said in a 1951 interview. "Common sense would tell him to go in for something else, if he would have peace of mind and job security."

Harper did indeed have both when he died of a heart attack on July 31, 1961.

At the time of his death, Harper had planned to attend Notre Dame's October 8 matchup with Northwestern. The 12–10 upset victory by the Wildcats over the eighth-ranked Irish certainly doesn't rate anywhere near Notre Dame's uprising against Army decades earlier, but it was a significant game nevertheless.

The loss was another embarrassment in the post–Leahy era funk and sent Notre Dame reeling. But it also got the school's brass thinking. This young Northwestern coach on the other sideline impressed them. It was the third straight time his team had beaten the Irish, and he would make it four in 1962.

Two seasons later, in 1964, Notre Dame hired Northwestern's Ara Parseghian, who helped the Irish rediscover the roots Harper had planted so many years before.

Strike a Pose

Humble Heisman Beginnings

Tim Brown figured he was well on his way toward a game-breaking play the first time he ever touched the football in a college game, when everything went blank. Then a freshman, Notre Dame's eventual seventh Heisman Trophy winner had been told earlier in the week that he would be eased into the Irish lineup for Notre Dame's 1984 season opener with Purdue in Indianapolis.

"The coaches knew that down here in Dallas, I had never played in front of more than a couple of hundred folks," recalled Brown, an alumnus of Dallas's Woodrow Wilson High School. "But when [coach] Gerry Faust is giving his big speech in the locker room, he ends it with, 'Tim Brown, I want you to return the opening kickoff.' I was just shaking in my pants, man."

So shaken was Brown that he forgot his helmet in the locker room and had to run back to get it. That was the last vivid memory of the opening moments of his collegiate football career.

"I can honestly say I don't remember what happened," he said with a chuckle. "All I know is they squib kicked the ball to me. I remember getting over to it and getting my hands on it. And I saw a hole and started running. It was weird, because I'm like, 'Why isn't anybody trying to tackle me?' At some point. I must have dropped the ball. I must have freaked out, went into shock or something, because I have no recollection of fumbling the ball. I know I didn't get hit. I finally turned around, and it was like, 'What happened?' What a way to start your career."

Brown certainly ended it in style, though, taking home college football's top individual prize in 1987.

Humble beginnings is the common theme for all seven of Notre Dame's Heisman winners.

John Huarte (1964) earned his first letter at Notre Dame *after* winning the Heisman. He had barely played as a junior or sophomore, and no freshmen played in that era.

Paul Hornung (1956) had to endure a coaching change—the legendary Frank Leahy to the mortal Terry Brennan—after his freshman season, as well as an extremely inexperienced supporting cast his senior year and two dislocated thumbs in his final game in an Irish uniform.

John Lattner (1953) was told he wasn't fast enough or flashy enough to make it at Notre Dame by friends and neighbors in his Chicago West Side neighborhood. He also had to overcome five fumbles his junior season in a game against Purdue and the wrath from Leahy that came along with it.

Leon Hart (1949) was so fired up when he was called into his first Notre Dame game, he collided with a team-mate on his way from the sideline to the huddle.

John Lujack (1947), meanwhile, was thrust into action in game seven of his sophomore year when 1943 Heisman Trophy winner and starting quarterback Angelo Bertelli was called up by the Marines just before Notre Dame's showdown with third-ranked Army in '43. Lujack then had to face eighth-ranked Northwestern, number two Iowa Pre-Flight, and powerful Great Lakes to finish the season. He then missed almost three years of school, including two football seasons, serving in the Navy during World War II.

Bertelli (1943) had to learn a new offense in 1942, when Leahy bagged the old Notre Dame box for the T-formation. Then he didn't even think he would play in 1943 due to an imminent call-up by the Marine Corps during World War II.

But beginning with Bertelli, Notre Dame has forged a Heisman tradition unparalleled by any other school. Not only has an Irish player won the trophy on seven different occasions, since the tradition was started by the Downtown Athletic Club in 1935, but heading into the 2004 season, Notre Dame has had three players finish second (Bertelli in 1941, Joe Theismann in 1970, and Raghib Ismail in 1990).

Five Irish players have finished third (Bill Shakespeare in 1935, Lujack in 1946, Nick Eddy in 1966, Terry Hanratty in 1968, and Ken MacAfee in 1977). Four finished fourth (Creighton Miller in 1943, Ralph Guglielmi in 1954, Tom Clements in 1974, and Tony Rice in 1989), and seven finished fifth (Bob Williams in 1949, Lattner in 1952, Hornung in 1955, Jack Snow in 1964, Ross Browner in 1977, Vagas Ferguson in 1979, and Reggie Brooks in 1992).

Angelo Bertelli, Quarterback, 1943

Angelo Bertelli was already a month into basic training at Parris Island, South Carolina, when Notre Dame's dream season of 1943 came to a bitter end.

The Springfield, Massachusetts, product had been the starting quarterback for the first six games of that season for the Irish, but a call-up by the Marines just before Notre

Dame's showdown with number three Army in Yankee Stadium thrust sophomore John Lujack, an eventual World War II veteran and Heisman Trophy winner himself, into the spotlight.

The Irish averaged 43.5 points in the Bertelli-led games, and the Irish knocked off number two Michigan in Ann Arbor (35–12) and number 3 Navy (33–6) in Cleveland, Ohio, along the way.

Lujack had filled in nicely, leading Notre Dame past three top ten teams (Army, Northwestern, and Iowa Pre-Flight) heading into the season finale with Great Lakes. Bertelli was able to listen to the Great Lakes game on the radio and started crying when Great Lakes rallied with a 46-yard pass from Steve Lach to Paul Anderson with thirty-three seconds left on the clock for a 19–14 upset.

"When I was crying, they called me to the orderly room for a telegram," Bertelli told *South Bend Tribune* columnist Joe Doyle for a 1998 series in *Irish Sports Report*, a year before Bertelli died of brain cancer at his home in Clifton, New Jersey.

The telegram was to let the Marine lieutenant know he had won the Heisman Trophy. Although Bertelli wasn't exactly sure what that meant, his tears of despair quickly turned to tears of celebration.

The celebration got even better when Bertelli found out the Associated Press poll made Notre Dame the national champion anyway, despite the late loss to Great Lakes. Iowa Pre-Flight finished number two in the polls, followed by Michigan at number three, Navy at four, Purdue at five, and Great Lakes at six. Purdue was the only team behind the Irish in the final top six that Notre Dame didn't face.

Bertelli's season stats were modest by today's standards. In six games, he completed a total of 25 passes in 36 attempts for 512 yards. Ten of his 25 completions went for touchdowns, though, and his .694 completion percentage was outrageous in an era when 50 percent was considered well ahead of the curve.

"He's the best passing quarterback I was ever around in college or the pros," said Lujack, the 1947 Heisman winner.

Bertelli easily defeated Penn's Bob O'Dell and Northwestern's Otto Graham in the Heisman voting. Irish running back Creighton Miller was fourth, and left tackle Jim White was ninth.

Bertelli had finished sixth in the voting in 1942, when he threw for 1,039 yards but with a modest .453 completion percentage. In 1941, he finished second to Minnesota halfback Bruce Smith. Bertelli threw for 1,027 yards that year as a single-wing tailback and actually led the nation in passing.

"I never thought I'd be playing at all in 1943," Bertelli said. "Coach Leahy even let me play baseball [the previous] spring instead of spring [football] practice. I was sure I'd get called by the Marines before then."

Leahy caught another break when star halfback Creighton Miller returned from a brief Army call-up because of high blood pressure.

Actually, Leahy initially didn't think he was ever going to get a chance to coach Bertelli. Leahy was the head coach at Boston College when Bertelli was a senior at Cathedral High School in nearby Springfield, but Leahy couldn't convince Bertelli to stay close to home.

Bertelli had to sit out as a freshman in 1940 per freshman ineligibility rules, but by the time he was eligible to play in '41, coach Elmer Layden had resigned, and Notre Dame had hired Leahy. Leahy, meanwhile, had been watching Stanford and the NFL's Chicago Bears have some success with the T-formation, and he decided that Bertelli would be a perfect fit for it in 1942.

The first run with the T produced a 7–2–2 record, so there weren't big expectations for 1943. Notre Dame had also lost quite a bit of talent to military call-ups. But it all fell into place, even when Bertelli did get the in-season call-up to the Marines.

What Bertelli couldn't do in 1943 was attend the Heisman Trophy award presentation in person. He, in fact, had to pick up the trophy in late December when he had a pass.

"It wasn't much of an affair," Bertelli said of the missed event. "It's not like the TV extravaganzas today. Besides, I was a real skinhead, shaved bald rather than a buzz cut. I wouldn't have looked good on TV."

John Lujack, Quarterback, 1947

There was never a gnawing feeling that World War II would not end and that John Lujack's college football days really were over. But the Notre Dame quarterback was keenly aware of the worst-case scenarios of war.

"If I was OK physically, I always planned on coming back to Notre Dame," said Lujack, who went into active duty in the Navy after his sophomore year in college. "It was always in my heart."

Several other schools tested that notion, though. While Lujack and coach Frank Leahy were both in the Navy during the 1944 and '45 seasons, the Connellsville,

Pennsylvania, product received overtures from several Irish rivals, trying to get him to transfer.

"Nothing doing," Lujack told them. He had also turned down an appointment to West Point when he was a senior in high school, which shocked and even angered some of the people in his hometown. "But Notre Dame was the only place I ever wanted to go," he said emphatically.

Lujack and Leahy had hit it off from the start. Angelo Bertelli, the eventual 1943 Heisman winner, had established himself as the starting QB when Lujack showed up as a freshman in 1942. So his first opportunity to shine came on defense.

Leahy had the Irish freshmen scrimmage the varsity the first day of practice, and Lujack continually throttled the progress of Notre Dame's new T-formation offense.

"Leahy stopped practice to see who made the tackle," Lujack recalled. "I told him that I did. After a couple more times of this, he stopped bringing practice to a halt, and he stopped asking who made the tackle."

Lujack filled in for Bertelli in the final four games of the 1943 season, when Bertelli got called up to the Marines. In a 26–0 throttling of Army, he threw for two scores, ran for one, intercepted a pass, and punted. His only blemish on the day was a missed extra point.

"Not bad for a guy who had to beat out three all-state quarterbacks and an all–New England quarterback," Lujack said. "Of course, I never made all-state myself. I was all-county. But, as my friend Creighton Miller likes to tell people, we were the only school in the county. Well, we weren't the only school, but I let it go, because he got such a big kick out of it."

Lujack, in turn, got a big kick out of showing off his

athletic prowess during his sophomore year. Because he was not expected back for the 1944 football season, Lujack didn't have to go through spring drills. So he went out for the basketball team and became a starting guard. And he went out for the baseball team and the track team, and became the first four-sport letterman at Notre Dame in three decades.

"I don't think anyone's done it since," Lujack said. "And it wasn't easy. At my first baseball game, I got two singles and a triple out of four times up. Then between innings, I went over to the track and won the javelin and tied for first in the high jump. My roommate, who was a pretty jovial guy, said to me afterwards, 'Hey, if you get dressed real quick, I think I know somewhere where there's a swimming meet.' "

When Lujack returned from World War II for the 1946 season, his focus was strictly football. He threw for 778 yards as a junior and rushed for 108 more, but his most memorable play came on defense when an open-field tackle of reigning Heisman Trophy winner Doc Blanchard helped preserve Notre Dame's 0–0 tie with Army.

Lujack ended up third in the Heisman balloting that season behind another Army standout, Glenn Davis, and Georgia's Charlie Trippi, while Notre Dame won the national title with an 8–0–1 record.

The Irish ripped through their final three opponents of the season by a combined 94–6 count and ended up leading the nation in total offense, rushing offense, total defense, and scoring defense.

The 1947 season was even better. The Irish never trailed in any game during that season, and only Northwestern came within two touchdowns. For his part,

Four Heisman Trophy winners and All-American Creighton Miller pose with then-head coach Bob Davie in the summer before the expanded Notre Dame Stadium's 1997 grand reopening. From left are Leon Hart, Johnny Lujack, Davie, Paul Hornung, John Huarte, and Miller. (Courtesy South Bend Tribune)

Lujack improved his completion percentage from 49 percent to 56 percent. Forty-two players on that squad ended up playing pro football, including Lujack. He eventually returned to Notre Dame to coach quarterbacks during Leahy's final two seasons.

"I had read about the Heisman and knew about it, but it didn't have all the hoopla it does today," Lujack said. "I'm not sure I ever knew at the time what it meant to win it, but I do now. I can get introduced to people as having played for Notre Dame, and that doesn't seem to strike them much. But then somebody says, 'He won the Heisman Trophy.' *That* seems to impress them."

Leon Hart, Right End, 1949

At Leon Hart's funeral in September 2002, amid the celebration of a life that had touched so many so deeply, some of the former Notre Dame All-American's closest friends were shocked to find out he played football at all, much less was one of the most storied players at the mecca of college football.

"He was the same way with us kids," said his son Kevin, who played on a national championship Irish team himself (1977). "He was so low-key about his football career. He downplayed it more than anything else. If somebody would bring it up, he'd quickly change the subject. I never, myself, saw game film of him until I was in my thirties. I just always knew him as being a really good father."

The elder Hart's football career was hardly forgettable. One of only two linemen ever to win the Heisman, Hart, originally from Turtle Creek, Pennsylvania, was a four-year contributor under coach Frank Leahy and carried the distinction of having never played on the losing side in a college game. The Irish went 36–0–2, winning three national titles, during Hart's career (1946–1949).

"His graduating year [1950] and my graduating year [1980] were thirty years apart," Kevin Hart said, laughing, "so our reunions were always at the same time during the summer. And his teammates would be all high and mighty. They considered the guys in my class punks. They scoffed that we could win a national title with a loss. God, it was really funny. I loved those guys."

And Leon Hart's teammates loved him from the start, even though he was just seventeen years old when he showed up at Notre Dame in the fall of 1946, while many of them were seasoned World War II veterans. Hart, however, was physically dominating from the start, in part due to having worked his high school summers in the steel mills near Pittsburgh.

He was the number two defensive end as a freshman, but from 1947 on, he was a starter at right end on both sides of the ball. In his Heisman Trophy–winning season, Hart (995 points) easily outdistanced runners-up Charlie Justice of North Carolina (272) and Doak Walker of Southern Methodist University (229) in the voting. Teammates Bob Williams and Emil Sitko finished fifth and eighth, respectively.

Hart didn't rack up big numbers. His best statistical season came in 1949, when he had 19 catches for 257 yards. But he was a punishing blocker on offense and a nightmare to block when he played defensive end. He also lined up at fullback from time to time, amassing 112 yards on 22 career carries and a TD.

And he did all of it while wearing the wrong size shoes for four years.

When Hart was a freshman, the Irish equipment manager asked him how big his feet were. He replied they were size fourteens. But the equipment manager refused to give him fourteens and made him wear thirteens instead.

"I think part of it was the equipment manager didn't believe him, and part of it was he didn't want to go to the extra trouble of getting him fourteens," Kevin Hart related. "Back in those days, anything larger than thirteens had to be specially ordered. They had to extend the soles. So thirteens it was."

Coincidentally, both Kevin and Leon's grandson Brendan (Kevin's oldest child), who walked on at Notre Dame, wore size thirteens. "And they were big shoes to fill," Kevin said, "more so for what he did away from football."

Leon Hart, who went on to three all-pro seasons among his eight with the NFL's Detroit Lions, almost didn't end up at Notre Dame.

"Bear Bryant had sent him a one-way ticket to visit Kentucky," Kevin Hart related. "But his high school coach warned him about it, saying that a lot of coaches who did that wouldn't give you a ticket back home if you didn't sign. You'd have to call your parents."

The University of Pittsburgh, several California schools, Tulane, Maryland, and most of the Big Ten schools all went to great lengths to impress Leon to get him to sign with them, even offering round-trip tickets.

Then there was Notre Dame.

Hart took a late train from Pittsburgh to South Bend and arrived after midnight. Edward "Moose" Krause, the eventual longtime Irish athletic director who was Notre Dame's line coach at the time, was supposed to pick up Hart at the train station but forgot. Hart woke Krause up out of a dead sleep with a phone call, and Krause apologized profusely.

"They brought Leon back to the barracks they had for the ROTC people," Kevin Hart related. "It was these Quonset hut–style dorms. And they stuck him in there about two in the morning. Well, about three in the morning, one of the veterans came in and kicked Leon out of his bed.

"But the next morning, Moose and Frank Leahy talked to Leon. They were very honest with him, even if they didn't take very good care of him. And Leon liked that. The low-key approach worked with him. The honesty did, too. It was how he lived and how he died. He knew he was doing things right."

John Lattner, Right Halfback, 1953

The most publicized stretch of adversity in John Lattner's otherwise storybook existence at Notre Dame was the Purdue game of his junior year, in which he lost five fumbles. But the most painful episode was losing his father his freshman year.

"It was a real setback," Lattner recalled. "But that's when you found out what a really great school Notre Dame was and the great support they had. I'm a Catholic kid, and I believe in God and believe in praying. And I believe in going down to the Grotto and saying, 'Hey, I need help.' It may sound goofy, but I asked my dad for support, too. It was tough, but I survived."

And then thrived.

Lattner wasn't great at any one thing, but he was good at everything. He punted. He returned kicks and punts. He played defense. He ran the ball. He caught passes. He even played basketball.

In fact, during his sophomore collegiate season, the former basketball captain of Chicago city champion Fenwick High had his moment in the spotlight at Madison Square Garden against eighteenth-ranked New York University.

"There were 18,000 people there, and the game had gone into overtime," Lattner said. "Everybody was on the edge of their seats, but me. I'm at the end of the bench looking at the girls and the bookies. In those days, guys were betting all the time. It was a lot different than it is now. Well, I'm watching all the action and not paying a bit of attention to the basketball game, and all of a sudden I hear assistant coach Johnny Dee scream out, 'Lattner!!' "

There were nineteen seconds left in the game, and Lattner was having trouble getting out of his sweat clothes. Finally, he was in the game, and the clock was in single digits.

"We were losing by a point, and I'm not sure how the ball got to me," he said. "I was around the top of the circle. No one came to guard me, so I said, 'What the hell, I'm going to shoot it.' It went in, and we won by a point, 75–74."

The next day, renowned New York journalist Red Smith wrote a piece about two-sport athletes, featuring Lattner.

"[Teammate] Leroy Leslie gets on me about him playing forty-some minutes and scoring twenty-two points and getting nothing in the paper," laughed Lattner. "Here I scored two points and got the headlines. He called me a name that I won't repeat, but he wasn't really mad."

Leahy sure was, though, when Lattner fumbled five times, as Purdue and Notre Dame combined for 20 in a 26–14 Irish football win back in 1952.

"Twenty?" Lattner reflected. "It seemed more like 29 or 30. The funny thing was, it was a gorgeous, sunny day. The weather conditions were perfect. It couldn't have been any better."

Lattner temporarily avoided Leahy's retributions by driving back to Chicago with his brother after the game rather than taking the train with the team back to South Bend.

Finally, during a team meeting that Monday, fate caught up to Lattner.

"Leahy gets up on stage and says, 'Oooohh my God, lads. There is a traitor, there's a young lad who matriculated from a fine high school, who fumbled five times against the enemy,' " Lattner related, sounding every bit like Leahy in inflection and tone. "Leahy went on, 'He disgraced us, the Notre Dame coaches and his teammates. He also disgraced Our Lady of the Golden Dome.' Leahy didn't mention my name, but I knew I was the one."

After the meeting, Leahy asked Lattner if he was having girl problems. "I told him, 'No, coach. I'm not having girl problems or boy problems,' " Lattner related.

Then Leahy wondered aloud whether Lattner was involved with gamblers. "He thought maybe I was trying to throw the game," Lattner said. "Truth is, I knew the bookies in Chicago, but I never bet money with any of them. We beat the spread by two points anyway. And coach believed me."

But the punishment wasn't over. Lattner had to go out to the practice field on his day off and run under a rope tied across the H-shaped goalposts. After about 500 times of this, Lattner couldn't get under the rope anymore. He ended up hitting it with his face and breaking it—the rope, that is.

Leahy also wanted Lattner to confess his "five deadly sins" to a priest. Lattner never did do that, but he did carry around a football everywhere he went for a week per Leahy's orders.

"My teammates even put a handle on it for me as a joke," Lattner said. "I went into my classrooms, and the professors laughed their butts off. It worked out good. They felt sorry for me. They didn't know who I was before, but they did now."

Name recognition helped Lattner as much as anything else during his Heisman run in 1953. He had finished fifth in the voting as a junior. Despite not leading Notre Dame in rushing, passing, receiving, or scoring that season, he edged out Minnesota's Paul Giel in one of the closest ballotings in history.

"Paul Giel was really the prominent halfback in the Midwest at the time," Lattner said. "I mean, he was a hell of a halfback. I think one of the things I was fortunate about was that we played on the West Coast, East Coast, down in Texas, so we got a lot of coverage. Our sports publicist, Charlie Callahan, did a heck of a job. I won the Heisman Trophy because of him."

The Irish did receive some national championship consideration that year, but not from the two wire service polls. Notre Dame, derailed by a late-season tie against twentieth-ranked Iowa, finished number two in the AP poll.

Leahy had collapsed earlier that season during a showdown with Georgia Tech and missed two other games before announcing his resignation roughly six weeks after the season's end.

Lattner attended the Heisman festivities with his mother, who had never been to New York City or been aboard a plane before in her life. "Mae had a great time," Lattner remembered. "I wish my dad could have been there, too. But we stayed out till 3:30 in the morning the night before the presentation. It was a great memory I'll always keep with me."

Paul Hornung, Quarterback, 1956

For most of his youth, Paul Hornung was convinced basketball was his calling. Even when it became apparent that football was the ticket to his dreams, he still didn't want to let basketball go.

Kentucky football coach Paul "Bear" Bryant picked up on this. So while Bryant was trying to recruit the Louisville Kentucky, Flaget High multisport standout, he enlisted the help of Wildcat basketball icon Adolph Rupp.

"I was all-state in basketball in Kentucky and had about ten scholarship offers," said Hornung, who has since relocated back to his hometown. "Then when Adolph Rupp tells me I can come out for basketball, that was quite a statement."

Hornung also liked the fact that the Southeastern Conference had decided to let freshmen be eligible, while Notre Dame was sticking to having first-year players sit out.

"I was almost assured I was going to play as a freshman at Kentucky," Hornung said. "I really didn't know a lot about Notre Dame. I didn't follow them like a lot of kids did at that time. I really didn't know much about that. But my best friend and my mother sure did. Those were the two forces that really got me up there."

Hornung never did get a chance to play in a game for the man who recruited him, Frank Leahy. But the two formed a bond that continued into the Terry Brennan era.

"It was a pain in the butt to sit out as a freshman," Hornung said. "But Leahy was so good to me. He'd bring me up with the varsity in practice and have me punt and kick off. And he really did more for me publicity-wise than anybody at Notre Dame. He really made some fantastic remarks about me when I was a freshman. That's when the publicity really started."

It eventually led to the first and only Heisman Trophy to be won by a player on a losing team, when Hornung edged out Tennessee's Johnny Majors in 1956. It also led to some friction between former coach Leahy and new coach Brennan throughout Hornung's career.

Hornung embraced both men and downplayed the transition of changing coaches and systems after his freshman season. Then again, this is the same guy who played his final collegiate game with two dislocated thumbs, prompting a switch to halfback, and downplayed that.

"I played fullback, too," he said rather proudly. "You had to do it. They just tape you up and go. Today's players would take four weeks off. There's no way they'd play under those conditions. They'd be too worried about their future."

Hornung faced much tougher obstacles growing up, particularly the absence of his father in his life.

"My mother and father got divorced when I was one," Hornung said. "So I didn't have a dad. But luckily this wonderful man named Henry Hoffmann came into our lives. He wasn't a relative of my mom or mine, but we called him 'Uncle Henry.' And he was like a father to me. He really took care of me. I trusted him with my life. He was always by my side. He was the most honest man I've ever known, a man of very high character, just a sweetheart."

And Hoffmann was a regular at Notre Dame for Hornung's games.

Hornung broke into the lineup all over the field as a sophomore, although he played behind All-American Ralph Guglielmi at quarterback, and he even fulfilled his hoops dream, playing on the Irish basketball team as a sophomore.

"That was really fun," said Hornung, who averaged 6.1 points a game. "I wanted to go back out as a junior, but Terry Brennan wanted me to concentrate on my studies, so I wouldn't fall behind. So that's what I did."

Hornung then went on to a phenomenal junior year, the highlight of which was a 17–14 victory over Iowa. Hornung rallied the Irish with a touchdown pass, then not only got Notre Dame into field-goal range to go ahead with 2:15 left to play, he kicked the winning field goal.

"I won a lot of votes and national honors in that game," said Hornung, who finished fifth in the '55 Heisman voting. "Then something happened that was very unique. I got carried off the field. Terry Brennan, though, grabbed me after the game and said that had never happened at Notre Dame and he didn't want to make a habit of it. I said, 'OK, I understand.' "

In 1956, it was Hornung's turn to do the carrying. The Irish, short on both seniors and scholarship players, began the year at number three in the polls. A season-opening loss to SMU (19–13) dropped the Irish to number seventeen. After a win over Indiana and a home loss to Purdue, the Irish fell out of the polls for the balance of the season. Notre Dame finished 2–8, with its only other victory coming in dramatic fashion against North Carolina (21–14).

But the Golden Boy, a nickname fashioned by Irish trainer Gene Paszkiet, was nothing short of golden during the otherwise disastrous season. He completed 59 of 111 passes for 917 yards, though he did throw 13 interceptions to just three TDs. Hornung ran for 420 yards, caught three passes, returned punts, returned kickoffs, kicked extra points, and was impressive on defense.

"I didn't think I had that great of a year," said Hornung, who went on to play professionally with the Green Bay Packers. "I had some outstanding games, but I think my junior year must have won it for me, because it came as quite a surprise."

John Huarte, Quarterback, 1964

Twenty-one-year-old John Huarte fidgeted in a hospital bed, staring at the phone and hoping it would ring.

He had just been told by three South Bend doctors that his injured throwing shoulder would require surgery the next morning. Huarte had suffered the injury during a spring in which he emerged almost out of nowhere to beat out nine other quarterback candidates for the starting job.

Teammate Harry Long had tackled Huarte hard during that day's spring practice session in March 1964, driving Huarte's shoulder hard into the turf. To that point, the spring sessions had been nothing short of a dream with new coach Ara Parseghian. Under previous head coaches Joe Kuharich in 1962 and Hugh Devore in 1963, Huarte didn't play enough to earn a letter. But his confidence remained strong.

"I remember when we played at Northwestern in '62 and Ara was the coach and he had a quarterback named Tommy Myers," Huarte said. "I didn't get in the game, but I was watching intently from the sideline with my teammate Jack Snow. Myers would roll out and complete a pass, and I'd say, 'I can do that.' Then he'd do something else, and I'd say, 'I can do that, too.' Ara was such a great coach, and you could see that. I remember wishing he was my coach."

Wish granted. But suddenly, Huarte was in need of more wishes. Surgery surely meant his senior year would be wiped out and all that depth chart climbing would be a footnote in a nondescript career. So Huarte picked up the phone and called Parseghian, hoping for a little consolation.

What he got instead was something much better.

"When I told Ara they were going to operate, he said, 'The hell they are.' " Huarte recalled. "I felt, like well, this is kind of neat. My coach is taking a stand for me."

Parseghian had assistant coach Tom Pagna drive Huarte to Chicago to see a specialist. X-rays were taken, and the Chicago doctor had Huarte hold some sandbags. After a few minutes of that, the doctor told Huarte that inserting a pin into the shoulder and having surgery would be a huge mistake.

"It was a complete reversal from what I had expected," Huarte said. "It was one of the first times in my life I almost fainted."

In the coming months, it was the college football world that would almost faint at the recurring coming-out party of Huarte and his teammates. The Irish had gone 2–7 the previous year, but this season they ripped off nine straight wins before suffering an upset loss, 20–17, at USC in the season finale.

"I didn't know I was even up for the Heisman until about the eighth game of the season," said Huarte, who, along with Hart, were the only Notre Dame Heisman winners not to have finished in the top ten the previous year. "I finally saw my name bandied about, and I thought, 'That's really great.' But then I quickly went back to my original philosophy—just concentrate on today's game, on today's practice. That's what got me there in the first place."

Huarte completed 56 percent of his passes during his Heisman run and threw for 2,062 yards, which obliterated the old single-season passing standard at the time. Sixty of his 114 pass completions that season went to classmate and fellow Californian Jack Snow, who won All-America honors as well and finished fifth in the Heisman voting himself.

In between the Irish were Tulsa's Jerry Rhome in second place, Dick Butkus of Illinois in third, and Michigan's Bob Timberlake in fourth.

"We had a lot of the same players in 1964 that we had in 1963," Huarte said. "The difference was Ara Parseghian. It comes down to management and organization—putting people in the right places. In my own business, we had a guy who was really struggling at the order desk. We gave him a shot at sales, and he became a star. That's what Ara did."

Getting Huarte to South Bend in the first place wasn't difficult. Huarte was from a Catholic family and attended a Catholic high school (Mater Dei in Santa Ana). His older brother, David, went to Notre Dame and loved it. So did Huarte's high school coach.

"I was raised on a farm in California," said Huarte, the son of a minor-league baseball player. "I was one of those kids who sat out in an irrigation ditch in the fall and listened to Notre Dame football on the radio with my dad in an old beat-up truck. My imagination would just wander. And I would think, 'Boy, if I could ever play at Notre Dame.' That's how the candle was lit. Of course, I had no idea where Notre Dame was."

The football world was starting to forget where Notre Dame was before the breakthrough '64 season. In the post–Frank Leahy era, beginning in 1954, the Irish had gone a collective 51–48 under Terry Brennan, Kuharich, and Devore. That included five nonwinning seasons in a row (1959–1963).

"The real genius was the astute ability of Tom Pagna and Ara Parseghian to build an offense around the skills of their players," said Huarte, who went on to play eight pro seasons. "They were very good at that. I was in the right place at the right time. It wasn't about me. It was about the great leadership we had. Otherwise, we would have been just another team you forgot about."

Tim Brown, Flanker, 1987

Of all of Notre Dame's Heisman winners, Brown was the first to really deal with the celebrity of it during the Heisman-winning season.

Even going for small errands became arduous, as well-wishers and autograph-seekers became relentless in their adulation. Brown lost 12 pounds due to the emotional wear and tear as much as, if not more than, the physical grind.

"The hardest part was that it all caught me by surprise," said Brown, a flanker/return man who showed much of the same versatility in his game that the early Irish Heisman

You Say Theezman, I Say Thizeman

Roughly a decade after he retired from Notre Dame and more than three decades after the fact, Roger Valdiserri still fields a barrage of phone calls every November.

"It's not a rumor," the former longtime sports information director and assistant athletic director said. "Every bit of it is true."

It is Joe Theismann's 1970 Heisman Trophy campaign. When the quarterback arrived at Notre Dame in the fall of 1967 from South River, New Jersey, his last name was pronounced THEEZ-man, but eventually it became THIZE-man to rhyme with Heisman.

"The funny thing, it wasn't just Joe who was affected by this," Valdiserri said. "The whole family goes by the THIZE-man pronunciation now."

It started innocently enough when Theismann was running onto the field for spring practice his freshman year. Valdiserri proclaimed, "There goes Joe

winners showed. "I mean, I went to Notre Dame for educational purposes. I never thought about playing pro football. I never dreamed of winning the Heisman. And I played two years for Gerry Faust on average teams.

"But then Lou Holtz comes in before the 1986 season, and everything changes. It really started picking up after my junior year. He started telling people that I was the most intelligent player he had ever been around and all those good things. It sort of piqued people's curiosity. Everybody

THIZE-man." He was corrected by friends of the Theismann family, Joe and Mary Hickey, but Valdiserri continued to push the pun.

"I said, 'No, it's Theismann, as in Heisman.' "

Joe Doyle, then the sports editor at the *South Bend Tribune,* picked it up and put it into one of his columns. It didn't gain national attention, though, until two years later, when *Sports Illustrated* was digging through the old clips and came across Doyle's column.

From then on, Joe THIZE-man it was.

The mythology in the story came in the form of how much money Notre Dame supposedly spent on Theismann and its other Heisman hopefuls over the years.

"My philosophy was not to spend an extra cent," said Valdiserri, who instead relied on his media savvy and the national demand for information on Notre Dame to drive the Heisman machine. "A lot of people had videos and gimmicky things, but I'm not sure you change a voter's mind with that. I think my job was simply to call attention to the player, and let his play speak for itself."

Theismann's play spoke loudly, but not enough to beat out Stanford quarterback Jim Plunkett for the award In 1970. Mississippi quarterback Archie Manning was third.

"I told my kids, what they're going to write on my tombstone is, 'He changed Joe Theismann's name,' " Valdiserri said with a laugh. "I worked at Notre Dame a long time. I guess this is what I'm going to be stuck with being known for."

wanted to know who this kid was. They had been watching Notre Dame football for the previous couple of years, and they hadn't seen this kid Lou Holtz was talking about."

Brown's junior-year numbers were actually slightly better than his Heisman season, but teams started to play keep-away when he was a senior. For instance, during the first four games of the 1987 season, Brown had eighteen punt returns, but over the last seven regular-season games, he totaled just sixteen.

Heisman Trophy winner Tim Brown cuts upfield during Notre Dame's January 1, 1988 Cotton Bowl loss to Texas A&M in Dallas. (Courtesy Joe Raymond)

After making a spectacular TD catch over two defenders in Notre Dame's season-opening 26–7 victory over Michigan, Brown leaped into the front-runner's spot for the Heisman with two spectacular punt returns in roughly a two-minute span against Michigan State.

The first was a 71-yarder for a TD in which he threaded his way through the coverage. But the second, a 66-yarder, caught even Brown by surprise.

"We were actually trying to block the punt on the second one," Brown said. "I was just hoping to get a ball that I could fair catch. I had no intentions of returning it. I ended up not putting up the fair catch sign, but I did start to run toward the sidelines. I was tired from returning the last one, because Michigan State went three-and-out. But I figured, why don't I just cut it up once? When I did, there was no one in front of me but the punter. If you look at me in film, I'm almost walking it into the end zone, because I was just dead tired. But it was all worth it. I don't think I would have won the Heisman without that game."

Brown easily outdistanced Syracuse quarterback Don McPherson and Division I-AA sentimental favorite Gordie Lockbaum of Holy Cross in the voting.

What a lot of people didn't realize is that Brown played much of the season with a shoulder injury and the last half of the season with a broken finger.

"The shoulder was a real problem at times," Brown said. "I remember jacking my pads up. It got to the point where the first hit I took every game, I would have to come out of the game afterwards. But once I got the adrenaline flowing, I was OK."

If it wasn't for a little ingenuity on Brown's part, he would have never played football in the first place, much less won a Heisman Trophy.

Growing up in Dallas, Brown was drawn to music and basketball. He could dunk by the time he was 5'11", but when his growth spurt stopped at 6', so did his basketball career, for all intents and purposes.

Ironically, during Brown's time at Notre Dame, he and his team won the 662-team intramural Bookstore Basketball Tournament, knocking out Holtz's team in the fourth round.

Football lured Brown away from the school band during his high school sophomore year, but he had to sneak onto the team, pretending to be at band practice when he was really playing football. The scam was discovered when Brown's mother received a call from the Roosevelt High School band director, wondering where her son had been.

Brown's mother, Josephine, finally relented, but was so worried about her son getting hurt, she never saw him play in person in high school or college. Brown's pro football career, which began in 1988, stretched longer than any of Notre Dame's previous Heisman Trophy winners.

"To this day, she has come to one game in the pros," said Brown following the 2003 NFL season. "That was a couple of years ago, when I got my one thousandth catch. I wish she could come to more, but I understand where she's coming from.

"My family has kept me grounded. They are very religious people, so football has always been secondary to them. From their standpoint, it doesn't matter what you do. It matters how you serve God. In a way, it makes me approach the game with a workmanlike attitude. I respect the game, but I don't idolize it. And I think that has made a difference in my life."

In Black and White

Transcending Racial Barriers

R oughly a decade and a half had passed since Wayne Edmonds and Dick Washington quietly, subtly made history and became the first black men to play football and letter in the sport for Notre Dame. But suddenly it all seemed so distant, almost like it had never happened.

Roughly a week and a half had passed since Alan Page helped will Notre Dame's football renaissance to completion. The All-America defensive end was a central figure in coaxing the Fighting Irish to a 9–0–1 season under then-third-year coach Ara Parseghian in 1966. Page and the other Irish players would have to wait until after the bowl games—from which Notre Dame was still abstaining—for it all to become official. But with exams winding down and the holidays coming up late in '66, the first imminent Irish national championship in seventeen years had the campus teeming with euphoria.

Yet in the quiet moments, Page couldn't escape the feelings of loneliness and isolation.

"Notre Dame certainly was a great place to play football," Page, a justice on the Minnesota Supreme Court since 1993, reflected. "But being an African American on campus back then was somewhat limiting. I can't remember exactly how many, but I know there weren't many people of color."

Page, in fact, is the only black player pictured in the 1966 Notre Dame football media guide. All the coaches are white, as are the administrators, support staff, and featured past heroes. Notre Dame didn't track the ethnic makeup of its student body consistently prior to 1974, the last year of the Parseghian era (1964–1974), but it's safe to assume the percentage of black undergraduates on campus was lower than the 2.2 percent charted for that year. By 1983 the figure has risen to 3 percent, with 3.5 percent in 1993 and 3.6 percent in 2003.

"I think Notre Dame is improving as far as diversity is concerned," Page said. "They're working at it, and they're stumbling too, just as, quite frankly, many colleges and universities in this country are. But I think they've made some progress."

At least the football media guides show people of color in all areas now, including a recent boost in the athletic administration. And at least there is a healthy respect for players of all backgrounds.

In the '66 guide, the Notre Dame players' ancestries are mentioned in their individual bios. Quarterback Terry Hanratty, for example, was listed as being of Irish-Italian ancestry. Halfback Rocky Bleier was of Irish-French-German descent. Defensive back Nick Rassas, who would go from walk-on to All-American, was of Irish-Greek descent. In fact, more then half of the Fighting Irish team was at least part Irish extraction.

For Page, however, no ancestry was listed. Perhaps it was a step up from the 1965 season, in which both he and senior Dick Arrington were listed as being of "Negro descent."

The world around Page and Notre Dame was certainly changing during that 1966 national championship run. The Civil Rights Act of 1964 and the Voting Rights Act of

Notre Dame had a formidable defensive front during its 1966 national championship run. Alan Page (far left) was joined by Kevin Hardy, Pete Duranko, and Tom Rhoads in this 1966 spring practice photo. (Courtesy South Bend Tribune)

1965 gave teeth to the swelling rhetoric that had been building steadily since the administration of Dwight D. Eisenhower in the '50s. Even Notre Dame president the Reverend Theodore M. Hesburgh was a key player in all of this, serving as the U.S. Commissioner on Civil Rights under presidents Eisenhower, John F. Kennedy, and now, in 1966, under Lyndon B. Johnson.

But life at Notre Dame for Page and other black students seemed to be stuck in a time capsule. It wasn't so much a matter of blatant discrimination as it was the ignorance of the era. It wasn't so much locked doors as it was closed ones. The education system failed most black Notre Dame hopefuls well before they got to the admissions process, yet the school was not part of the solution, either.

"In any institution, there is a top echelon of leadership—a president in the case of Notre Dame," said Thomas Broden, once a longtime professor at Notre Dame's law school and to this day a champion of civil rights. "People on the outside think they can press a button and everything changes. That often is not the way it works.

"The campus was substantially white in those days. There were some minorities in various positions, working on the grounds and things like that, but essentially it was an all-white and overwhelmingly male institution. It had been that way ever since the school was founded. Institutions are slow to change. There has to be something to jolt the institution into considering some sort of modification."

Page couldn't provide that jolt while a student at Notre Dame, but he did continue to fuel his own dreams during his four years on campus.

He had started the dream while growing up in Canton, Ohio, a city that built a shrine to football at its highest level—the Pro Football Hall of Fame—where, in fact, Page would be enshrined after a brilliant fifteen-year pro football career. But Canton was also a place where too many dreams, even those boosted by collegiate football scholarships and NFL cups of coffee, went to die.

"As early as I can remember, I have memories of football players who were great on the athletic field and didn't perform very well in the classroom," Page said.

"Many of them would go off to college on a football scholarship, and two, three, four years later end up back in Canton, hanging out on the street corner, unemployed and unemployable."

This helped reinforce the mantra Page's parents had been repeating since all their children had been old enough to hear it: Education is the key to a better life. And that was the gift they wanted to give their kids.

Money went only so far, with Page's father involved in running a bar and operating a juke box business around town, while Page's mom worked as an attendant at an exclusive country club. But the love and the lessons were so plentiful and so accepted in the Page household, Alan decided by the time he was in the fourth grade that he wanted to change the world by being a lawyer. A short time later, he found out football could accelerate that dream.

"From the time I first started playing football, I recognized that, for whatever reason, people looked at me differently, simply because I was an athlete," Page said. "They want your autograph. They want you to come speak, that sort of thing. Over time, you begin to recognize that you can take that and do something positive with it."

And that, in turn, led him to Notre Dame.

It was the academic reputation of the school, not its football tradition, that attracted Page. Diversity—or the lack thereof—wasn't going to be an issue in his mind. Whatever racial insensitivity he might encounter, if any, wasn't scary enough to convince him to take an easier path.

"So many people say and think that when things have been a certain way for a long time, they will always be that way, and they do this in regard to flaws in our education

Willingham Takes the High Road to Diversity

He was almost halfway into his first season as Notre Dame's head football coach when the first press conference finally passed without Tyrone Willingham being asked if the upcoming game carried any social significance.

Since becoming the school's first black coach in any sport on New Year's Day 2002, Willingham was continually poked and prodded on the issue, but never seemed to find a comfort level with the amount of attention it garnered nor any of the many tangents that sprang from it.

Perhaps he summed it up best at his introductory press conference when he said of his hiring, "Is this significant? Yes, I'd say it is significant. But I am first and foremost a football coach at the University of Notre Dame. The young men will expect me to be the kind of leader that they expect their fathers to be. And that's the role that I will try to go for."

system all the time," Page said. "But I never accepted that. There wasn't a single watershed moment. It's something I grew up with. I also grew up with the thought that those of us who have the ability have some obligation to do what we can to change what has always been. Just because it always has been doesn't mean it has to always be."

Page was like a lot of his white teammates in the recruiting class of 1963, in that football was secondary in

That's not to say diversity issues aren't near to his heart. They're just distant from his daily discourse.

Willingham is well aware that in the half century that has gone by since Wayne Edmonds and Dick Washington became the first black players to suit up for the Notre Dame football team, progress in the area of diversity at the school still needs attention. Even in the 1990s and into the new millennium, many of the black Irish players still felt a sense of disconnect. After all, they make up roughly a third of Notre Dame's total black male student population.

To his credit, athletic director Kevin White began diversifying the athletic department well before he hired Willingham.

"I've been very pleased with the position that our administration has taken in terms of addressing the diversity issues," Willingham said. "Like most universities, there's still a long way to go."

Willingham, though, knows the spotlight is more on him than on Notre Dame as a whole, meaning that other colleges may use his experience as a litmus test for their future coaching hirings.

"It's unfortunate that based on race, based on religion, based on a lot of things in this country, that we judge many by one," he said. "That is unfortunate. It all should be done on an individual basis. Tyrone Willingham should not necessarily reflect every African American. That's important. But if I can do anything to help make the situation better, then I'm delighted to do so."

their minds when they chose the school. Joe Kuharich, who went 17–23 in four years with the Irish (1959–1962) had recruited them. But only weeks after they had formally committed and weeks before spring practice would start, Kuharich parachuted out of Notre Dame and into a job as the NFL's supervisor of officials.

Freshman coach Hugh Devore was named interim coach, and the Irish went 2–7 in 1963, capping their fifth straight nonwinning season, and feeding a frustrated fan base that wondered whether football was important in Notre Dame's grand scheme of things anymore.

The administration answered with the hiring of Parseghian, who helped turn Notre Dame around in one season. The Irish went 9–1 in 1964, Page's sophomore season, 7–2–1 in 1965, and 9–0–1 in 1966. The Irish were number three in the final AP poll of 1964, number nine in 1965, and number one in '66. The Irish finished in the top fifteen every one of Parseghian's eleven seasons, but it wouldn't be until around 1970 when the Irish roster had more than five black players on it.

"It was difficult to recruit black players during that time," said former Irish assistant Tom Pagna, Parseghian's right-hand man on offense for all eleven of his seasons at Notre Dame. "The admissions standards were a problem, and then there was the lack of social life for minority students. Fortunately, there were people in the community who tried to help, and it did finally make a difference."

At the top of the list of those supportive in the South Bend community was a man named Arthur Hurd. He lived just south of the Notre Dame campus until his death in 2003. But he was a beacon for the black players all the way back to the days when Edmonds and Washington came from western Pennsylvania and broke through at the end of the Frank Leahy era.

"You heard of Leahy's Lads? Well, we were Art's Boys," Edmonds said proudly. "All the Notre Dame players who were black got to know Art. He'd help them feel at home. He'd call them up and invite them over, and his wife would cook dinner. Every once in a while, he'd take you to a Bears game in Chicago. He was our anchor then in the '50s, and

I know he was that for guys like Alan in the '60s, too."

Edmonds has his own theory as to why Notre Dame was slow to recruit black players, beyond the legitimate barriers of admissions and culture shock.

"From what I've heard and from my own ideas, I'm not sure some people at Notre Dame were sure whether recruiting black players was a good thing or not," Edmonds said. "I think they were afraid of losing their strong southern support, money that they had been given. It's something that pulled at me for some time."

It didn't pull as much at Page, though. He knew someday, whatever the problem was, he wanted to focus on the solutions.

Playing pro football wasn't part of the solution, but it did provide resources, open up avenues, and give Page a name. And the first-round draft choice seemed to be good at whatever he tried following graduation from Notre Dame in the spring of 1967. In 1971, for example, he ventured into drag racing and beat a national record on his first official try on a drag strip. He drove his own purple Dodge Charger 97.08 miles per hour at the Minnesota Dragways. Less than a year later, on January 6, 1972, he became the first defensive player ever to be named Most Valuable Player in the NFL.

In 1979, he became the first active NFL player to complete a marathon (26.2 miles), and eight years later he completed a 62-mile race.

Along the way, he kept the promise he made to himself as a fourth grader and enrolled in law school while still playing with the Minnesota Vikings. He graduated from the University of Minnesota law school in 1978, three years before his pro football career ended.

It was during that last year in law school, though, when all the ideas, all the hopes, all the drive began to crystallize from one humbling episode.

"We had a new line coach with the Vikings that year," Page related. "He thought the best way to teach me, Jim Marshall, and Carl Eller to be better football players was to read the team playbook to each other at night."

There were nine of them in the group at the time, and Page discovered that four of his defensive line teammates couldn't read.

"I was always troubled by the conflict between athletics and academics," Page said. "This experience focused me on the experience that what I was seeing was an academic problem, not an athletic problem, because each of these young men had gone to some of the nation's finest postsecondary academic institutions, and each one of them graduated.

"They didn't miss out on learning how to read there. Each one had graduated from high school, so they didn't miss out on learning how to read there. I learned how to read in the first, second, third grade. I dare say that's when most people learn it. My Viking teammates weren't athletes then. It pinpointed to me that what we were dealing with was an academic problem. It was one of those moments that helped clarify how at least I could begin to do something to have an impact."

He hasn't slowed down since. Perhaps his most visible contribution is the Alan Page Foundation, which he and his wife, Diane, established in 1988. The first group of Page "scholars" went into action the next year. The Alan Page Foundation, in growing numbers of both students and dollars each year, provides financial assistance to young men and women of color pursuing their education beyond high school.

"Probably the most important part of it, at least from my standpoint," Page said, "is that we require our grant recipients to go back into their communities—either where they came from or where they're going to school—and work with young children as tutors and role models and mentors, to send a message to those young children to change their attitudes about education. We want to let them know that education is important and that with education, they too can be successful."

The Alan Page Foundation primarily benefits students who attend colleges in Minnesota, but there is an arm of it in practice at Notre Dame as well.

"Even though my years at Notre Dame were not easy ones," Page said, "it was an important part of my life. I want to give something back to that community, because all in all, I think it's safe to say my time at Notre Dame turned out well."

Edmonds looks back at his career at Notre Dame in a similar light, as a time when he took advantage of his educational opportunities, as a time when he realized just how good of a football player he could be when the field was leveled, as a time when his aspirations grew wings and took off.

That's not to say there wasn't injustice splashed in his face on a regular basis. He couldn't, for instance, even get a haircut on campus. And when the team traveled to play the University of North Carolina in 1953, his sophomore season, the former tackle had to stay at a Catholic parish, because the team hotel didn't allow black guests.

"I could go on and on about that, but the point is that I had been through all that stuff before, and that would have happened wherever I went to school," Edmonds said. "My buddies at Pitt ran into the same things when Pitt went to play in the Sugar Bowl. But coach Leahy and all the other coaches were great. When schools threatened to boycott Notre Dame if they brought their black players with them, Leahy stood right up to them. And on the practice field, Leahy and the other coaches treated everyone the same—nasty."

Actually, Edmonds grew quite close to Leahy and assistant coach Bob McBride. He also felt liked and respected by his teammates. And that helped him move past the bigotry and intolerance that surfaced away from the football field.

Edmonds came to Notre Dame from Canonsburg, Pennsylvania, a town in Washington County, south of Pittsburgh. Dick Washington grew up just 42 miles away in the mining town of Vanderbilt. The two didn't know each other before showing up in South Bend and had no idea whether there would be other black players or students on campus.

The first black students to enroll and graduate from Notre Dame came in the 1940s, two decades after Notre Dame students clashed with the Ku Klux Klan in South Bend over their anti-Catholic sentiments. In the 1920s, Indiana was thought to have the most powerful Ku Klux Klan presence in the country. Much of its activity was in the central and southern part of the state, but it had fingers that reached up north toward South Bend. And it wanted to establish a presence there to curb what it perceived as a dangerous rise in Catholic prowess.

Roughly 4,000 Klan members gathered in South Bend on May 17, 1924. Starting that afternoon and moving deeper into the weekend, Notre Dame students and local townspeople stood up to the bigotry, forcing many of the Klansmen back onto the trains on which they arrived. Others were beaten and their robes shredded. Finally, Notre Dame president Matthew Walsh and Irish football coach Knute Rockne called for an end to the violence. The

Tim Brown, here in action against Pittsburgh in a 1987 matchup at Pitt, was Notre Dame's seventh Heisman Trophy winner, but the first African American to win from the school. (Courtesy Joe Raymond)

KKK was repelled and soon went into decline in Indiana.

But racial intolerance and inequity lived on, even in the supposedly enlightened North. Edmonds had grown used to it, but he never accepted it. Neither did black Irish basketball players James Bertrand and Entee Shine, who preceded Edmonds and Washington to Notre Dame by a year. Nor did Aubrey Lewis, a halfback from Montclair, New Jersey, who followed shortly thereafter.

Some, like Edmonds, stayed all four years and graduated. Some did not.

"I learned to live with difficult things," said Edmonds, who includes Leahy's successor, Terry Brennan, in that "difficult" category. Brennan was Edmonds's coach in 1954–1955. "And I learned no matter how bad things got, if people are going to fall, well, I'm going to be the last one standing."

Things did get bad for Edmonds after he graduated from Notre Dame, but never bad enough to undo all the good he did. Instead of playing pro football, he went on to get advanced degrees in psychiatric social work from the University of Pittsburgh.

"When I was a kid, I wanted to be a good person who worked with the community and worked to help people do better," Edmonds said.

Wherever his career path took him, he was able to accomplish that. He helped integrate swimming pools, restaurants, and hotels back in his home town. He raised money for the NAACP and started a local chapter. He was one of the organizers who helped bring Dr. Martin Luther King Jr. to Pittsburgh.

"We'd get all sorts of calls," Edmonds said. "They'd say, 'We're going to bomb you. We're going to shoot at your car,' that sort of stuff."

But the threats melted away, and Edmonds never did. He took early retirement in the late 1980s and lives in Harrisburg, Pennsylvania. He celebrated his seventieth birthday in October 2003.

In his own quiet moments, he reflects back on the experiences of black Notre Dame players like Page in the '60s and Lewis in the '50s and wonders if racial progress is coming fast enough for the present-day Irish.

"The one thing that ties us all together was we came to Notre Dame for the same thing," Edmonds said. "We wanted to play football *and* we wanted to get a good education, get one step ahead in life. That's why we came. And that's why I'm still glad I came."

The House That Rockne Built—and Built Again

The water from the dozens of overflowed toilets reached ankle deep in some places, while the St. Joseph, Indiana, County Health Department was closing down fifteen concession stands in Notre Dame Stadium. Then there were the roughly 150 people treated for heat exhaustion on a muggy 82-degree day while watching an Irish football team that was a twenty-point favorite struggle to a four-point escape.

It's hardly what Knute Rockne had in mind when he drew up plans for a new football stadium to open in the fall of 1930. Then again, this wasn't 1930. It was September 6, 1997, the day an expanded and refurbished Notre Dame Stadium was christened, however shakily.

Notre Dame had added roughly 21,000 seats to the structure, not to mention faster elevators, permanent souvenir stands, meeting rooms, fancy landscaping, and, of course, more toilets.

The $53 million expansion brought the seating capacity to 80,795, up from 59,075 in the old configuration. Notre Dame went from forty-fourth among college football stadiums in size to fifteenth. The original number of seats listed during 1997, the first year of the expanded stadium, was 80,225. But that was based on computerized seating projections made during the construction phase of the project. Eventually, the capacity number was modified to 80,012, then 80,232, then to its correct and current listing of 80,795.

It took twenty-one months to finish the expansion and four years to clear up the resulting lawsuits that sprang up in 1999 from the embarrassing and expensive flooding of the main concourse on Reopening Day. (Repairs were reported to cost $4 million.)

"There's a certain amount of anxiety with a project of that magnitude," then–university vice president the Reverend E. William Beauchamp proclaimed—and that was before the toilet fiasco caused by a combination of design flaws, low water pressure, and outdated commodes.

[The stadium expansion] looked good on paper, and in reality, it's even better," said Beauchamp, who has since moved on from Notre Dame and is now the president of the University of Portland. "One of our main goals was to preserve the look and feel of the old stadium. I think we were successful in doing that. It's still very intimate. We still have the collegiate bowl design. People walk in, and they still feel like they're in Notre Dame Stadium. It's just bigger."

Knute Rockne—Notre Dame's head football coach from 1918–1930 and its athletic director, business manager, track coach, ticket distributor, equipment manager, and uniform designer at various points in between—did envision a stadium expansion. In fact, he made sure then Notre Dame president the Reverend Charles L. O'Donnell mentioned it to the press when the university unveiled its plans to the public in 1929. The thought was that an upper deck or decks could be added to bring capacity to 135,000 someday.

Had Rockne had his way, though, the original would have seated 100,000 — roughly the size at the time of Michigan Stadium, which was erected in 1927 by the same design firm, the Osborn Engineering Company of Cleveland, Ohio. Interestingly, Fielding Yost, the former legendary Wolverines head coach and athletic director of that era and beyond, had campaigned for a mammoth 300,000-seat structure in Ann Arbor, Michigan.

Rockne lost a lot of stadium battles, too. Just getting the Notre Dame powers-that-be to replace old Cartier Field was a decade-long struggle for him.

Cartier, at best, could squeeze 27,000 fans into it. Located just north of the current stadium site, the Irish football facility wasn't big enough to attract big-time teams on a consistent basis. That, in turn, created scheduling problems for Rockne.

Notre Dame was a big draw on the road and could reel in big money by doing so, but playing road games in that era wasn't just a matter of facing the inconvenience of travel and hostile crowds. The officiating at the time was thoroughly corrupt. The home team was in charge of paying the referee, who was often a local writer. Those referees-writers, in turn, were often paid under the table to promote the game in which they would officiate. The alliances, more often than not, resulted in favorable calls for the home team at critical junctures.

Rockne eventually learned to play that game, too. Early on in his coaching career, he enlisted a *Chicago Tribune* writer named Walter Eckersall to officiate Irish games, paying him well over the market fee. The two became friends off the field and allies behind the scenes.

Murray Sperber, who uncovered crates of Rockne correspondences in the subbasement of the Hesburgh Library while writing his 1993 book *Shake Down the Thunder*, followed the long and deep connection between Rockne and Eckersall.

"I was sort of stunned when I put it all together," Sperber said. "It doesn't fit the Saint Knute image, but Rockne had to swim with the sharks without bleeding when he came into this system."

Perhaps the most controversial call involving one of Rockne's teams came during the most famous game of his era. It was Notre Dame versus Army in 1928. The Irish had already sustained two losses on the season, and if it had been the twenty-first century instead of the 1920s, Rockne would have been eaten alive in the Internet chat rooms and on sports talk radio.

The coach dug down into his psychological bag of tricks for the meeting between the two teams at Yankee Stadium and delivered his famous "Win One for the Gipper" speech.

After falling behind 6–0 in the third quarter, the Irish roared back for a 12–6 advantage with the go-ahead TD—a halfback pass from Butch Niemiec to reserve Johnny O'Brien—coming with 2:30 left in the game. However, Army stormed down the field, thanks in part to a 55-yard kickoff return, and was on the 1 foot line ready to score when the whistle blew, reportedly prematurely, ending the game.

"Army protested the call, but the ref kept saying, 'It's over. It's over.'" Sperber said. "And who was the referee with the quick whistle? Walter Eckersall. It wasn't even a

Home Cooking

How Notre Dame's coaches have fared in Notre Dame Stadium:

YEAR	COACH	RECORD	WINNING PERCENTAGE
1930	Knute Rockne	5–0–0	1.000
1931–1933	Heartley "Hunk" Anderson	7–4–1	.625
1934–1940	Elmer Layden	25–5–0	.833
1941–1943, 1946–1953	Frank Leahy	37–6–2	.844
1944	Ed McKeever	4–0–0	1.000
1945, 1963	Hugh Devore	5–3–0	.625
1954–1958	Terry Brennan	16–8–0	.667
1959–1962	Joe Kuharich	10–10–0	.500
1964–1974	Ara Parseghian	51–6–1	.888
1975–1980	Dan Devine	25–7–0	.781
1981–1985	Gerry Faust	16–11–0	.593
1986–1996	Lou Holtz	51–13–1	.792
1997–2001	Bob Davie	24–7–0	.774
2002–present	Tyrone Willingham	8–4–0*	.667

* Heading into the 2004 season.

Former Notre Dame coach Knute Rockne, a spokesman for South Bend automobile company Studebaker in the 1920s, poses with a Studebaker in 1927 as he addresses a group of Fighting Irish football players. (Courtesy South Bend Tribune)

home game, and he ended up helping the Irish. Imagine how Notre Dame lore might have changed. No one would have ever heard about the Gipper speech. It would have been just another speech that didn't work. So Rockne was a very shrewd guy and kind of a natural entrepreneur."

Indeed, Rockne turned college football at Notre Dame and beyond into big business, even without a large stadium. He knew it could be bigger, though. Many programs around the country took inspiration from the dollars Rockne was pumping into Notre Dame and built big stadiums of their own.

In the neighboring Big Ten alone, Ohio State opened Ohio Stadium in 1922. Michigan State, not a member of the Big Ten at the time but an aspiring Midwest power nonetheless, followed with Spartan Stadium in 1923. Illinois (1923), Purdue (1924), Northwestern (1926), Michigan (1927), and Iowa (1929) all jumped on board and all still use those stadiums today. Wisconsin, incidentally, built Camp Randall in the pre-Rockne era (1917).

The resistance to a new stadium at Notre Dame came on several fronts. There was the philosophical dilemma that if Notre Dame built the stadium, it would raise doubts about the school being a serious academic institution. There was also the belief that Notre Dame needed new academic buildings on campus more than it needed a new stadium. Many of the old buildings were wooden firetraps.

"Rockne wanted to keep all the football money and reinvest it in football," Sperber said. "But the priests were heroes, because they took that money and built most of South Campus with it."

The biggest stumbling block turned out to be short-sightedness on the part of the administration. They figured there were only 3,000 students at Notre Dame. And if 5,000 or 6,000 townspeople came to the games, that would be considered a big gate. So why in the world would they need a stadium that seated between 50,000 and 60,000?

But one of Rockne's greatest gifts as a coach and athletic director was being a visionary. He not only saw the big picture, he could see beyond it. Notre Dame's national following was gaining momentum in the late '20s. Rockne envisioned subway alumni without the subways—vast numbers of fans driving to South Bend or taking the train.

Notre Dame's famous tunnel is prominent in this 1930 photo of Notre Dame Stadium under construction. (Courtesy South Bend Tribune)

Eventually when he designed the stadium, he included expansive parking lots in the plans.

As his vision continually stalled in the dream stage, Rockne threatened to go coach at other schools—Columbia, Wisconsin, USC, and Ohio State, to name a few—in order to leverage the new stadium. Finally, it worked. In 1927, the Reverend Matthew J. Walsh, the third of four presidents to serve during the Rockne head coaching era, appointed three committees to study the feasibility of a new stadium.

For good measure, Rockne submitted his resignation to Walsh and flirted with Ohio State to push things along. The Buckeyes had just forced Dr. John Wilce out of coaching

and back into private practice. When Rockne withdrew from the mix, Ohio State hired someone named Sam Willaman.

The cost of the stadium was originally tagged for $700,000, according to newspaper accounts, and came in with a final price tag of $750,000—about 1.4 percent of what the expansion cost 67 years later.

Revenue was raised for the project by the sale of ten-year leases on box seats. At least four home games per year were guaranteed in the lease, but there were hints that that could be increased to five. Those five-game home seasons rarely came to pass, however, until the 1950s—long after the seat leases had expired.

Fans who purchased the seat leases were also promised they could witness Notre Dame B-team games and local high school games in the stadium at no additional cost.

Old Cartier Field had to be torn down to accommodate the new stadium, so the Irish played every game on the road in 1929. It was a daunting task, considering the perils of road games at the time and that Notre Dame was coming off its worst season under Rockne — 5–4.

Rockne himself was stricken with phlebitis, an inflammation of the veins, in his legs and was gravely ill for most of that season. In fact, his doctors told him there was only a 50–50 chance of surviving if he tried to coach at all that season. But he did anyway, sometimes from a wheelchair on the sidelines, sometimes via telephone from his hospital bed.

The Irish ended up going 9–0 and gave Rockne his second national title, to go along with the Four Horsemen–driven championship of 1924. Assistant Tom Lieb bore the burden of Rockne's tasks when he was absent. But by the time the 1930 season rolled around and the new stadium was set to open, Rockne had returned to full health.

Rockne was somewhat of a superstitious fellow. For example, he considered it bad luck for him or his players to eat bananas on game day. Thus, it was of little surprise when he insisted the old, lucky sod of Cartier Field be transplanted to the new stadium.

Excavation for the new stadium began on October 29, 1929, along with the final surveys. Actual construction didn't begin until April 1930. When it was completed, the new structure measured half a mile in circumference and stood 45 feet high.

More than two million bricks, 400 tons of steel, and 15 cubic yards of concrete were used. The seats were made of genuine California redwood. Included in the press box that sat atop the west side of the stadium were telephones Rockne had ordered so that the coaches could communicate with their fellow assistants and Rockne on the field.

Prior to the stadium's unveiling on October 4, 1930, there had been widespread sentiment that the new facility be named Rockne Stadium. Rockne himself publicly quashed the idea, more an act of the reality of the situation than one of modesty. His constant butting of heads with the administration made it improbable. So did the fact that most buildings in that era were named after people, mostly priests, who had passed away.

So Notre Dame Stadium it became.

Tickets for reserved seats went on sale for $3.00 with box seats carrying a $5.00 price tag. Dedication cere-monies—with increased ticket prices ($5.00 for reserved, $7.00 for box)—were planned for Notre Dame's second game, against Navy on October 11, 1930.

One of Rockne's off-the-field strengths that contributed both to Notre Dame's rise in popularity and Rockne's own celebrity was his ability to massage the press. This was quite apparent in the early accounts of the games played in the new stadium.

For example, the 1930 season opener drew 14,751 fans, but the local *South Bend Tribune* printed that there were 25,000 onlookers that witnessed Jumpin' Joe Savoldi's 100-yard kickoff return, which helped the Irish survive SMU, 20–14. Savoldi still shares the school record for longest kickoff return for a 100-yard field.

The next week, 40,593 came to see the Irish crush Navy, 26–2. However, the *South Bend Tribune* trumpeted a crowd of 50,000—"more than double that had ever previously seen a Notre Dame game."

Rockne must have loved the reviews, particularly since he seemed to have his hands in every detail. For example, he enlisted 500 Boy Scouts to help with the traffic. He encouraged the police who were working the stadium to be as courteous as possible.

The one common thread that the stadium opener shared with its reopening sixty-seven years later was that it was an unusually hot day.

The police were congratulated in the media for routing 15,000 cars with not a single accident. Roughly 125 sports writers from across the country jammed the press box and gushed about the new facility and the many dignitaries and celebrities who attended the game.

As for the fans, one of the biggest cheers of the day was reserved for referee Fred Gardner's accidental trampling by two Notre Dame linemen. The *South Bend Tribune* reported that "almost everyone was sober." One inebriate, who wasn't, almost got evicted from the stadium, but the police gave up when the fans booed them.

Notre Dame's starting lineup that day included a right guard listed at 155 pounds (Bert Metzger was 149 by season's end) and only two players who weighed more than 195 pounds.

One player who was notably absent was a tackle by the name of Frank Leahy. In fact, Leahy, who reaggravated an old leg injury three days before the SMU game, was the only Irish player unavailable for the first two games. He ended up missing the entire season, which turned out to be a national championship run.

Leahy would later coach the Irish and become the

second-winningest coach in college football history—behind only Rockne—and evolve into a pivotal figure in Irish lore, though not as celebrated as Rockne.

Rockne himself got to coach only one season in the stadium. There was some speculation that he might retire in 1931 at age forty-three. In late March of that year, Rockne received a telegram summoning him to Los Angeles for two days of hectic business meetings. Some accounts even had him set to explore motion picture interests as well.

Rockne's wife, Bonnie, had a premonition about the trip and urged him not to go by air. But Rockne didn't see the point in wasting time getting out to the West Coast.

He boarded a train from Chicago to Kansas City, where he was to catch Transcontinental-Western flight 599 to Los Angeles after meeting up with his family.

Shortly after takeoff, the plane flew into a storm and almost turned back for Kansas City. Instead, the two pilots forged ahead. Moments later, the plane crashed in a field near Bazaar, Kansas, killing all eight people on board.

While the world mourned—as Rockne had become an international figure—the prospect of renaming the stadium after him surfaced again. The university's administration simply referred to Rockne's original statements about not wanting the stadium to bear his name.

There came a point when some critics unofficially named the stadium "Rockne's folly," though. The Depression of the 1930s threatened to turn the stadium into a white elephant wrapped in brown brick. In the sixteen seasons between 1930 and 1945, Notre Dame drew in excess of 50,000 fans eight times, even though there was only one losing season (3–5–1 in 1933) during that time

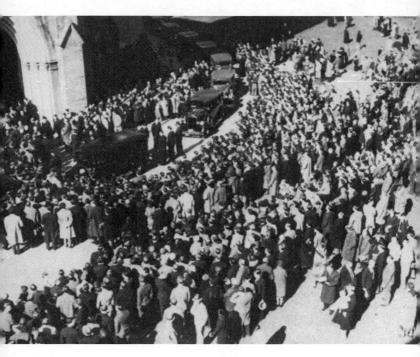

Mourners overflowed the Notre Dame campus for coach Knute Rockne's funeral in 1931. (Courtesy South Bend Tribune)

span. The Irish continued to be a huge hit on the road, however.

In 1932, home attendance dipped to 8,369 for the season opener against Haskell, then a stadium-record low 6,663 for Drake the next week. By contrast, 55,616 witnessed the road game at Pittsburgh that season, 78,115 came to Yankee Stadium for the Army–Notre Dame game that year, and 93,924 watched USC's 13–0 shutout of the Irish in Los Angeles.

It wasn't until the student population doubled in the

1940s, the economy recovered, and Leahy rebuilt the dynasty that the huge crowds Rockne had envisioned actually materialized on a consistent basis.

"Rockne's plans for a stadium that was bigger and more glorious than the 50,000 to 60,000 that Notre Dame eventually settled on was more ego than anything," Sperber said. "But the 50,000 model would eventually make sense. The roads and the railroads weren't so good to South Bend in Rockne's day. But the building of the stadium improved the railroads and improved the roads much faster than if no stadium had been built."

Rockne himself sort of morphed into mythology, even though his real-life details were infinitely more interesting and entertaining. The thought of renaming the stadium lay dormant until the 1990s, when expansion finally became a reality.

Notre Dame's largest crowd prior to expansion was 61,296 for a 24–6 loss to Purdue on October 6, 1962. Four years later, Notre Dame stopped counting turnstiles and based attendance on ticket sales, making the figure a constant 59,075.

Since that 1966 national championship season, only one home game hasn't been a sellout: a 48–15 rout of Air Force on Thanksgiving Day of 1973. The game was moved due to TV's wishes, and there were no students on campus. Official attendance at that game was listed as 57,236.

It was also in 1966 when Notre Dame revealed to the public that it had studied expansion but opted against it.

"Present facilities are not conducive to practical expansion without exorbitant costs," then–Notre Dame ticket manager Robert M. Cahill proclaimed in February, seven months before the team under coach Ara Parseghian began its national title run. "It would require building another stadium around the outer edge of the present one to have the foundation for an upper deck, which might increase the seating capacity by 30,000."

Ironically, when Notre Dame finally did decide to expand, that's pretty much the concept that was adopted. Two others models were submitted, both of which would have kept the renowned Touchdown Jesus mural on the Hesburgh Library visible. One was a horseshoe shape, with seats added everywhere but the north end zone. The other option was adding seats from goal line to goal line, but leaving the end zone seats alone.

"We quickly ruled out the first two options," said Beauchamp, the point man on the stadium project. "With 20,000 additional seats, we thought the stadium would be too tall. We wanted to preserve the old feel."

Bubba Cunningham, an associate athletic director during expansion and a business manager and ticket manager when expansion talks started to heat up, had been pushing for expansion since the early 1990s.

"It's funny, at one point in the process I found a letter from Moose Krause to an alum telling him not to worry, that expansion wasn't far off," Cunningham recalled. "I don't know exactly what year it was, but it was an old letter."

Krause retired as Notre Dame's athletic director in 1981.

Season tickets for alums have been determined by a ticket lottery since 1966. Each year Notre Dame sent an increasingly larger amount of money back to the lottery losers.

"I think one tipping point was in 1992, we sent back more money than we kept," said Cunningham, now the athletic director at Ball State. Another impetus had come in

An expanding Notre Dame Stadium under construction in April 1996.
(Courtesy Joe Raymond)

September 1991, when the national board of directors of
the Notre Dame Alumni Association adopted a resolution
encouraging the university to study the feasibility of
expanding the stadium.

Finally, it was when president Edward A. Malloy made
it one of his forty-three recommendations to the university's
trustees in May 1993 that the impediments toward expansion disappeared.

"There was a time that the thought of the demand
exceeding the supply was a good thing," Cunningham
said. "But the demand kept growing. Another big factor was
the stadium was going to need renovations anyway (about

Stadium Firsts

Here is a list of some of the firsts in the refurbished and expanded Notre Dame Stadium during a 17–13 Irish victory over Georgia Tech, September 6, 1997:

First TV timeout: 12:29 of the first quarter

First man out of the tunnel (after captains): Notre Dame's Kory Minor

First drop of a sure interception for a touchdown: Notre Dame's Kory Minor

First time the crowd did the wave: With 1:48 left in the game

First coin-toss verdict: Notre Dame won and elected to receive

First partial score to be cheered: Boise State, 17, Wisconsin 7, second quarter

First partial score to be booed: Georgia Tech 10, Notre Dame 7, second quarter

First flyover: 1:23 EST

First guffaw: An announcement of a moment of silence to honor, among others, "the recent death of Princess Grace" (In actuality, it was Princess Diana of Wales)

First whining about the lack of air conditioning in the press box: August 13, 1997, when the media first found out about it

First player to have the ball in his hands: Notre Dame's Allen Rossum on the kickoff return

First tackle: Georgia Tech's Dante Booker

First Notre Dame freshmen in the game: Linebacker Grant Irons, tight end Jabari Holloway, and running back Tony Driver

First pass reception: Notre Dame freshman Joey Getherall

First first down: Notre Dame, at the 13:36 mark of the first quarter on an Autry Denson 1-yard run

First touchdown: Notre Dame's Autry Denson on a 3-yard run with 4:45 left in the first quarter

First punt: Notre Dame's Hunter Smith, 48 yards

First punt of less than 10 yards: Notre Dame's Hunter Smith, 8 yards

First sack: Notre Dame's Corey Bennett dropping Joe Hamilton for a loss of 5 yards, 13:30 left in the second quarter

First Jim Sanson field goal: 25 yards, 9:48 mark of the first quarter, bobbled snap, wide left

First deficit: Georgia Tech 10, Notre Dame 7, 4:14 of the second quarter

First statistical surprise: Notre Dame quarterback Ron Powlus's 22-yard run

First sigh of relief from new Notre Dame head coach Bob Davie: Five minutes after the game

$25 million worth). It became apparent we could finance a lot of the renovation through new ticket sales."

The expansion project was financed by $53 million in tax-exempt bonds and unsolicited gifts. "Really, as it turns out, it will very much be a benefit to the academic programs," Beauchamp said at the time. "I said from the beginning we wouldn't touch any other fund-raising program. The additional revenue from ticket sales will be more than enough to pay off the bonds. It will also provide some additional revenue to be used in academics as well."

Ellerbe Beckett, which had designed many of the other buildings on campus, was signed on as the architectural firm. Ground was broken shortly after the 1995 season ended. Construction, performed by Casteel Construction Co., of South Bend, took twenty months, and the Irish were able to play in the unfinished stadium during the 1996 season, coach Lou Holtz's last.

The exterior of the old stadium was preserved inside its new shell. Outside, tan bricks were used to blend in with many of the other buildings on campus. Rather than lower the field, Notre Dame eliminated the field seats and the first two rows of permanent seats to improve sight lines.

Touchdown Jesus now disappears at about row 50 coming down from the top of the stadium. However, if Irish players need to see the famous landmark, they can walk down to the 15 yard line near the south end zone and peek through portal number 135.

Before expansion was complete, Notre Dame asked Miami of Ohio to bow out as the first opponent in the bigger stadium. As part of that concession, the Irish agreed to play Miami in basketball, home-and-home, in a four-game series. An ironic footnote, the RedHawks ended up beating the Irish the first three games—all by nine points or more—before Notre Dame edged Miami 70–69 in the series finale, December 8, 2001, in Oxford, Ohio.

Georgia Tech replaced the RedHawks on the football schedule. In Bob Davie's first of sixty games as Notre Dame's head coach, the man he would face on the opposing sideline, George O'Leary, was also the man who eventually replaced Davie when he was fired five seasons later. O'Leary himself left Notre Dame after less than a week due to fabrications on his résumé.

O'Leary and his heavy underdog Yellow Jackets almost spoiled Davie's coming out party on September 6, 1997. Davie had reveled in a rare outdoor pep rally in the stadium the night before that drew upwards of 35,000 people. But the Irish struggled mightily against Tech.

Even beyond the plumbing troubles, there were plenty of glitches off the field. Thousands of fans without tickets drove to the stadium to party in the parking lots, clogging the arteries to the stadium. The traffic was the worst in thirty years, according to South Bend police. Then just before kickoff, a band P.A. announcer misidentified Princess Diana of Wales as Princess Grace during a moment of silence.

On the field, it took two impressive fourth-quarter stops and a revived running game to keep Davie from becoming just the third Notre Dame coach since 1900 to lose his first game.

Autry Denson, who would later go on to become Notre Dame's career rushing leader, plunged in from 1 yard out with 2:37 left to cap a 69-yard scoring drive and provide the winning margin. Lineman Tim Ridder fell on Denson's fumble at the Tech 40 to keep the drive alive.

"Anytime you can win your first football game of the season, especially when you have a new coaching staff, that is a big, big win," said Davie.

Roughly 250 former Irish players formed a human tunnel before the game and looked on as the Irish prevailed. And somewhere, Rockne was likely watching too.

Declaration of Independence

Forging a National Identity

A s he lay in a hospital bed pondering the second medical miracle to befall him in a six month period, Mike Wadsworth's thoughts eventually drifted back to everyday affairs.

Even though Wadsworth hasn't worn the title of University of Notre Dame athletic director since February 2000, his untainted love for the school and his familiarity with the challenges it faces make it impossible for him to ever disconnect.

So there he was, just six months removed from surgery to help rid himself of bladder cancer and six days removed from a successful kidney transplant, perplexed at how his former employer and alma mater had worked its way back into serious discussions about conference membership for football.

The odds of such a seismic change of direction in the school's thinking seemed even more remote than Wadsworth's wife, Bernie, being a compatible donor for the November 2003 kidney transplant, which she indeed was.

"The doctors laughed when she first volunteered," said Wadsworth, four months before he lost his battle with a second wave of cancer. He passed away on April 28, 2004,

In a League of His Own

Mike Wadsworth knew the day would come when his only functioning kidney would fail, but he never really believed it.

Wadsworth, a defensive tackle for the Irish (1962–1965) and later the school's athletic director (1995–2000), can't remember much of his six-week hospital stay when he was six years old, other than the constant fevers, the loving reassurance of his parents, and the caveat the doctors delivered to his parents when it was all over. Wadsworth went about his life from that point as if it never really happened. When he matriculated to Notre Dame, the seriously infected kidney was basically useless as expected, but his other kidney worked just fine for the time being.

It was a recurring knee problem that limited Wadsworth from reaching stardom while a defensive lineman with the Irish. Yet upon graduation, Wadsworth not only played for the Canadian Football League's Toronto franchise for five seasons, he did it while attending law school full time and completing an eighteen-month bar admissions course. The Canada native was also named CFL Rookie of the Year when Notre Dame was winning the national title in 1966.

"I was married and had a family, so playing pro football was something I was willing to take a chance at, even with the injuries," Wadsworth said. "Eventually, the knee required more surgery after my fifth season, but I was done with law school requirements then and could get on with my life."

In everything he did, he seemed to overcome adversity. That was especially true in 2003, when Wadsworth first overcame bladder cancer, then successfully accepted a kidney transplant from his wife, Bernie.

In the aftermath of the transplant, the strapping Wadsworth harkened back to the words of his childhood doctors.

"The doctors warned my parents that I probably wouldn't grow up to be a very strong person," the man whose college nickname was "Moose" said with a heartfelt chuckle. "They kind of envisioned this little weakling who wouldn't be able to be involved in athletics or

Mike Wadsworth (left) chats with the Reverend James Riehle in the final seconds of ND's loss to Stanford, November 27, 1999 in Palo Alto, California. It turned out to be Wadsworth's final football game as Notre Dame's athletic director. (Courtesy Joe Raymond)

whatever. My family still jokes about it."

Even though the cancer came back in Spring 2004 and ultimately took his life, Wadsworth never stopped finding humor in the misprognosis; he is probably still smiling about it somewhere.

less than two months before his sixty-first birthday. "We'd heard the odds of a nonblood relative being a match at something like a million to one. Yet Bernie was so determined she would be the ideal match."

Notre Dame's potential as an ideal match for membership in the Big Ten Conference, meanwhile, had been dismissed by Wadsworth and others at Notre Dame just five years earlier.

"We had to ask ourselves the fundamental question," began Notre Dame president the Reverend Edward A. Malloy at a press conference — in London, of all places — on February 5, 1999. "Does the core identity of Notre Dame as Catholic, private, and independent seem a match for an association of universities — even a splendid association of great universities — that are uniformly secular, predominantly state institutions, and with a long heritage of conference affiliation?"

He was quick to add that "this wasn't an athletic decision." But in every successive statement made by Malloy, it was apparent the future of the Irish football program was a thread in each and every discussion.

The Notre Dame board of trustees took just ninety minutes to sort through the information and return a resounding no that February afternoon. Malloy had come to the same conclusion a couple of months earlier.

No one studied the issue harder than Wadsworth, though. Upon Wadsworth taking the job in 1995, one of his first calls went to Big Ten commissioner Jim Delany.

"I wanted to get in touch with him right away because of the interaction we had in football and otherwise," Wadsworth recalled. "I also just wanted to introduce myself and try to get things off to a proper start between the two of us.

"He had raised, at the time, that there had been some talk between Notre Dame and the Big Ten before and he was not particularly happy, because he thought when that initial conversation took place, that Notre Dame didn't give it the attention it deserved."

Wadsworth told Delany he had no idea about any of that, because his job prior to becoming AD at Notre Dame was serving as his native Canada's ambassador to Ireland. So he wasn't all that plugged into some of the issues involving Notre Dame athletics that hadn't previously surfaced publicly.

Wadsworth also wanted to get a better handle on what Notre Dame's recent union with the Big East would entail before delving into any discussions with other conferences. The Notre Dame program joined the Big East in the summer of 1994, beginning competition in the 1995–1996 season, in men's and women's basketball and most of its Olympic sports—such as baseball, volleyball, and swimming—but most decidedly not in football.

It was Wadsworth's directive to usher in that era of limited conference membership, particularly to revive the men's basketball program. The Notre Dame administration had long ignored former coach Digger Phelps's pleas to join the Big East, and that stubbornness to cling to independence eventually swallowed up both a rich hoops tradition and the long and stellar coaching career of Phelps, who was purged after the 1991 season.

Wadsworth got a taste of what conference life might be like almost immediately, sitting in on meetings in the somewhat dysfunctional Big East. The schools with Division I-A football in that league and those without it always seemed to be at odds.

Basketball was every bit the marquee sport of the
league, but it was football that contradictorily held the
union together as well as threatened to implode it.

"We didn't talk about it a lot in our meetings,"
Wadsworth said of the persistent sense of impending self-
destruction, "but there were always undercurrents."

In part because of that volatility in the Big East, in part
because of Wadsworth's respect for Delany, and in part
because Notre Dame no longer felt it could naturally tran-
scend any and every major change in the landscape of
college athletics (as men's basketball had shown), Notre
Dame agreed to examine the possibility of merging with its
Midwest neighbors. A public exchange of information and
seemingly goodwill began in April 1998, with Wadsworth

Notre Dame executive vice president the Reverend E. William Beauchamp (left) and athletic director Michael Wadsworth (center) look on as Bob Davie is introduced as the new Irish head football coach on November 24, 1996. (Courtesy Joe Raymond)

collaborating with several of Notre Dame's associate athletic directors at the time—primarily Missy Conboy, Tom Kelly, and Bubba Cunningham.

"Number one, we looked at the economics of it," Wadsworth said. "And we were able to satisfy ourselves projecting out as much as we could—six, seven years—that the economics were a wash. We actually found we might be at a slight disadvantage by joining, but those numbers become pretty spongy when you go out that far."

Many of the coaches of the various sports, meanwhile, were split. Then–football coach Bob Davie, at the time, publicly applauded the move to stay out of the Big Ten. But five years later, Davie, as a member of ESPN's college football multimedia family, suggested just as publicly that Notre

Dame should reconsider its stance, claiming that perhaps "arrogance" was what kept the Irish on an independent path for football.

Alumni and fans of the program, who overflowed Wadsworth's mailbox with letters, were avid in their support for independence at the time as well. And that factored greatly into the equation.

So did Notre Dame's identity.

"We looked at how a football program contributed to that identity and how that identity contributed to football," Wadsworth said. "We certainly had our down periods over the years when we haven't had high levels of success in football, yet we've always returned to one of the more prominent programs in the country. We've survived those dips as an independent.

"As an independent, we continued to have sort of a mythology that had been there all those years. We felt that was pretty vital to the kind of culture and reputation of Notre Dame. It served us in recruiting. It served us in television contracts. It served us well in terms of the type of endorsement values we could get. That's a unique position in college football."

Wadsworth and his committee felt that unique position was critical in recruiting to offset the smaller pool of available athletes who could meet Notre Dame's stringent academic standards.

"I still think the lifeblood of any college program is recruiting," Wadsworth said. "You've got to be able to get the kids, and you've got to give a coach an opportunity to do that, because ultimately it's going to be the talent on the field that's going to win games."

As Wadsworth got further into his research, what

seemed like a viable option at first increasingly took on the look of a wild gamble.

Former Irish coach Ara Parseghian, who coached at Northwestern in the Big Ten before beginning his brilliant eleven-year run at Notre Dame, came to Wadsworth to persuade him against the move. Parseghian mentioned that when he was in the Big Ten, Northwestern—the league's only private school—was too often on the wrong end of 9–1 votes. And he insisted that if the Irish became team number twelve in the numerically challenged league, Notre Dame would find itself on the wrong end of too many 10–2 votes.

"Ara said, 'Nothing against the big, state schools,' " Wadsworth related, " 'but they just operate and think differently.' "

So what changed in five years?

Three losing seasons in football—the most in any five-year period in school history; the Big East finally having to do the crisis management it always feared it might have to do someday; and whispers that Notre Dame's access to the big money, big exposure Bowl Championship Series games might get squeezed when the BCS contract ran out following the 2005 season.

Wadsworth couldn't fathom Notre Dame's protected position in the BCS ever getting displaced. The BCS had always been market-driven. And the bowls and TV networks loved the Irish. But what if the BCS shifted from a market-driven plan to one that more resembled the spirit and structure of the NCAA men's basketball tournament in selecting teams?

That's what crossed the mind of Wadsworth's successor, Kevin White, even though what ran through White's mind didn't find its way out of his mouth too often—at least around the media.

Meanwhile, the Big East lost members Miami, Virginia Tech, and Boston College to the Atlantic Coast Conference's aggressive expansion drive. The league reloaded with Louisville, Cincinnati, South Florida, Marquette, and DePaul; the latter two did not have football programs.

The new lineup souped up an already elite men's basketball conference but left football with even more volatility. In attendance, in stature, and in tradition, the three new football schools couldn't match the three departing schools. That put the Big East's protected BCS berth in jeopardy over the long term. That, in turn, raised the reality that the Big East's strongest football members—West Virginia, Syracuse, and Pittsburgh—could eventually scatter for new homes.

"Boy, I hope this works," said Gene Corrigan of the rebuilt Big East. In the short term, the Big East appears on solid ground, especially with the February 2004 decision to add a fifth bowl to the BCS mix. Then again, with the Big East, you never know.

Corrigan faced minimal conference debates during his time as Notre Dame's athletic director (1981–1987), but he was a proponent for expansion during his time as commissioner of the Atlantic Coast Conference. He tried unsuccessfully to get the league membership to court Penn State after Florida State was admitted. Penn State subsequently joined the Big Ten.

Corrigan remains as connected as anyone in college athletics through his consultant work and many longtime friendships and ties.

"Ever since the Big East has been involved in football, football has always been something that has threatened to blow the league up," he said. "It's a constant. I don't know

Former Irish athletic director Gene Corrigan answers questions at a press conference, January 28, 1983. (Courtesy Joe Raymond)

what else can be done, but I don't think this is necessarily happily ever after."

If the Big East crumbles, Notre Dame must find a new home for its basketball and Olympic sports. While Conference USA said it would welcome Notre Dame without football, neither the Big Ten nor the ACC figure to be so generous. And because Notre Dame has made such an investment in its other sports in recent years, being an independent in most of those sports is not an option.

But if Wadsworth had to do it all over again, he said he'd still come to the same conclusion: stay out of the Big

Ten or any other conference that required football be part of the package.

"Maybe things have changed beyond my scope of understanding," Wadsworth said. "But my concern remains if we have some down periods as a member of a conference, can Notre Dame retain its mythology?" he said. "If you're in the middle of the Big Ten for five or six years, what does that do to you? Does it hurt you more than being down five or six years as an independent? Do you become just another Midwestern school?

"I still think it's a huge risk with not enough to benefit for taking that risk. Notre Dame's development over the years was as a small school with a national following that kind of developed against all odds."

It was that very reputation that had Wadsworth excited about Notre Dame football while attending Catholic school in Toronto growing up. He even turned down a scholarship offer from Michigan State before he had one from Notre Dame in hand because of his admiration for the school.

Wadsworth was largely unaware at the time that Notre Dame had repeatedly begged to join the Big Ten during the first thirty years of the twentieth century and was repeatedly rebuffed. Initially, the rejections seemed to center on the Big Ten powers-that-be not understanding Notre Dame's hierarchical structure. Later there were rumors of Notre Dame circumventing the established eligibility rules, though it is thought most of that was to mask anti-Catholic sentiment.

Later, during the Knute Rockne era (1918–1930), the Irish football program became so powerful, many Big Ten schools didn't want to have anything to do with Notre Dame—but they always hid behind other excuses. So successful was Notre Dame under Rockne that, late in his run, sentiment among alumni and followers who wrote to the coach sounded a lot like the letters Wadsworth received some seven decades later.

Beating the odds, being independent, being a national presence became something to be proud of.

When Wadsworth enrolled at Notre Dame, the football program was in one of its darkest down cycles. The 1962 team went 5–5 under coach Joe Kuharich during Wadsworth's freshman season. That came on the heels of a 5–5 season the year before and a 2–8 campaign in 1960.

Kuharich parachuted out into the pro ranks in the spring of 1963, leaving the Irish to turn to interim coach Hugh Devore. Notre Dame went 2–7 that year before hiring Parseghian.

"You heard all the same arguments then as you did during the Gerry Faust era and that you're hearing now," Wadsworth said, "that the schedule was too challenging, that the academics were too restrictive, etc."

The only difference was there was no talk about joining a conference being a possible elixir.

"Of course, Ara came in the next year and turned all those discussions on their ear," Wadsworth said.

Until now.

White, once as outgoing as any athletic director in the country, has become reclusive during this time of self-examination for the Notre Dame football program. Occasionally he'll issue a short statement with "continuing to monitor the landscape of college athletics" consistently as its central mantra.

Until his death in April 2004, Wadsworth continued to monitor what Notre Dame did as a fan and not as a consultant.

But his hope was that those making the decisions remember what made the Irish program great over the long haul.

"When you're running a race, sometimes you stumble," Wadsworth had once said. "But life is about getting back up. It's how the race ends that counts. That's what you keep in mind."

The Holy Trinity

Hesburgh, Joyce, and Krause

T he sound of the phone ringing was more annoying than alarming at first for the Reverend Theodore M. Hesburgh on the morning of September 20, 2002.

The Notre Dame president emeritus was enjoying sleeping a little later than usual in his 10-foot-by-12-foot room in Corby Hall, his place of residence for more than a half century. He didn't even hear the sirens from the ambulance or the commotion in the hallway. He didn't smell the fear.

The voice on the other end of the phone shook, but the situation was clear. Something terribly wrong had happened to Hesburgh's right arm in business for so many years and his best friend in life, the Reverend Edmund P. Joyce.

"They found him on the floor in his room," Hesburgh reflected. "It was a sad thing."

Joyce, eighty-five years old at the time, had suffered a stroke. It would be weeks before he could move a foot on the paralyzed side of his body and even longer until he could move his hand. But Hesburgh made a point of visiting the Notre Dame vice president emeritus every day and making sure Joyce knew that their bond was as strong as ever.

They would talk about how divergent their political views still were and what wonderful journeys they took together, in endeavors on campus and on working vacations around the world. They would reminisce about how they

The Rev. Theodore M. Hesburgh (left), former longtime University of Notre Dame president, is honored at halftime of the 2002 Notre Dame–Pittsburgh football game in South Bend. With Hesburgh is Notre Dame assistant band director Larry Dwyer. *(Courtesy Joe Raymond)*

rose to the top of the University of Notre Dame leadership in the summer of 1952, when they were both thirty-five years old, and how they figured they'd serve a six-year term and move on with life. And then they'd laugh that it wasn't until 1987 that they finally walked away.

"We figured after our six years were up, we'd go back and teach," Hesburgh said. "It's like meeting a guy at the tape after he'd just run the 100-yard dash and telling him to keep running."

There was a third man at the head of Notre Dame athletics during most of the Hesburgh–Joyce era. But former athletic director Edward "Moose" Krause had died roughly two weeks before Christmas in 1992. Still, the memories were so thick, that Hesburgh and Joyce could almost hear his booming voice, see that gentle smile and slight limp, and detect a hint of cigar smoke.

"I think Ed Krause is one of the few people I've known in my life that you could legitimately call a saint," Hesburgh said. "That doesn't mean he didn't have his faults. He had a drinking problem, and he conquered it. He always had the problem of being big and powerful, but he never misused it.

"And then there was what he did with his wife, Elise. She had a terrible accident that made her very difficult, because a part of her brain was damaged. But Moose never gave up on her, never stopped showing her love. He went through that like a soldier and was just such a loving husband and father.

"Of all the people I've gotten to see in my life, if I could pick out one who certifiably is a saint, I'd say Moose Krause. Not some priest, not some bishop, not even some pope. But Moose Krause."

Krause's term as athletic director ran from 1949 to 1981, and the thought was his title was much more ceremonial than practical. Father Joyce was seen as the decision maker and Krause the ambassador in the arrangement.

"Moose *was* an ambassador, a great ambassador for the university," said Roger Valdiserri, a former longtime sports information director and associate athletic director at Notre Dame. "When I traveled with him, you'd walk through airports or hotel lobbies, and everybody recognized him. And he handled it so well.

"Yet some people thought that's all there was to him, that administratively he didn't grasp the national focus. But I was close enough to him to know he knew what the heck was going on. He also loved Notre Dame, and he made sure that everything was done right. I just think Moose was a great icon at the university."

Krause left his mark at Notre Dame in many ways even before his unparalleled run as athletic director.

Born Edward Krauciunas, the son of Lithuanian immigrants came to Notre Dame from the rugged Back of the Yards section of Chicago. While he was in high school, Moose got his last named shortened to Krause by his high school coach at Chicago De La Salle, Norm Barry, who struggled with both the pronunciation and the spelling of the longer Lithuanian version. That same coach, who incidentally was a football teammate of Irish legend George Gipp at Notre Dame, also stuck Krause with the nickname "Moose."

It was Barry who was instrumental in getting Krause to Notre Dame in the first place. Krause was working in the Chicago stockyards when Barry arranged a meeting between the powerful-but-nimble prodigy and Irish legendary football

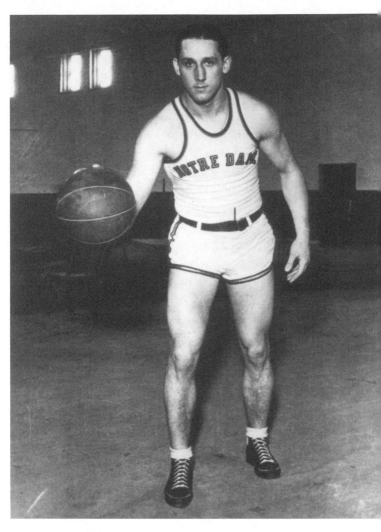

Edward "Moose" Krause was an All-America basketball player for the Irish, as well as an All-America tackle in football and a letter-winner in track, before becoming Notre Dame's longtime athletic director. (Courtesy South Bend Tribune)

coach Knute Rockne. Barry had played his final three seasons at Notre Dame (1918–1920) under Rockne.

Krause never got to play football for Rockne, with freshmen being ineligible at the time (1930), but the two did more than just quietly pass insignificantly through each other's lives.

During his freshman year, Krause received a failing grade on a science exam and was convinced there had been a grading error. His quest to have the matter looked into escalated to the point that Krause physically threatened a dean. The dean, in turn, arranged to have Krause expelled.

Krause was prepared to leave campus without any further displays of his temper. He stopped by Rockne's office to say good-bye and to say that he was sorry. Rockne offered to help set things straight, but only if Krause promised he would learn to manage his anger better.

Krause did learn to be a gentle giant off the football field. The dean did look into the possibility of a grading error and discovered Krause should have received a 78 rather than a 30. Rockne died later that school year— March 31, 1931, in a plane crash.

Krause went on to play football, baseball, and track at Notre Dame, but his biggest impact came in basketball. His career scoring average of 8.8 points is deceptive, given the low-scoring era and the fact that most games were still played on dirt courts. A typical winning score in those days for the Irish was in the thirties. And Notre Dame won a lot with Krause. The 6'3" center led Notre Dame to a 54–12 record in the 1932–1934 seasons and earned All-America honors all three years.

Purdue's John Wooden, who would go on to become a college basketball coaching icon, was the only player prior to Krause to be so honored. Heading into the 2003–2004 season, only sixteen others had earned consensus All-America honors in three seasons since Krause had done so. Additionally, Krause earned second-team All-America mention in football during the 1932 season.

Krause had an array of options after graduation in 1934, including a tryout with baseball's Chicago Cubs, but he chose to go into coaching instead. His first stop was St. Mary's College in Minnesota, where he served as head basketball coach and athletic director.

Eventually he ended up back at Notre Dame in 1942, as an assistant football coach under Frank Leahy. He also became an assistant basketball coach to his old head coach, George Keogan. When Keogan died suddenly at age fifty-three during the 1942–1943 season, Krause took over for his old mentor. He also coached the entire 1944 season in an interim capacity, then served in World War II as an intelligence officer with the Marine Corps.

He returned to Notre Dame for the 1946–1947 season and coached the men's basketball team for six more years, fashioning a 98–48 record, including 20–4 in his first non-interim season. Krause resigned after the 1951 season to devote more time to his athletic director duties (which started in 1949). Hesburgh and Joyce, incidentally, were just about ready to start their long run.

As athletic director, Krause helped raise almost all of the $8.6 million needed to build the Athletic and Convocation Center, which now bears Joyce's name. Opened in 1968, it was the first major athletic construction project since Notre Dame Stadium had opened for football in 1930.

Out of the spotlight, Krause was proud of the football schedules he put together, especially the degree of difficulty in them, which is a tradition that endures today. He was responsible for initiating the Miami series, which went dormant after the 1990 clash, and exhuming the Michigan series, which had ended after a 35–12 Irish rout in 1943 in Ann Arbor that left Wolverines coach Fritz Crisler vowing the two teams would never meet again.

Krause's most significant victories and accolades, however, came in his not-so-private life. After a drinking problem almost killed him, Krause not only joined Alcoholics Anonymous, he became a spokesman for AA and held meetings in his campus office.

Then there was his wife, Elise, who was not expected to live after suffering head injuries and broken bones in a taxi accident in January 1967, two weeks after their eldest son, Edward Jr., was ordained as a Catholic priest in Rome, Italy.

Elise Krause did live, but never again had a normal life. And as a result, neither did Moose. The injuries caused her to lose her ability to reason and control her emotions.

"She was such a lovely woman, but her personality changed," Hesburgh said. "She became very difficult to deal with."

In Elise's later years, Moose would spoon-feed her in the nursing home and sing her to sleep.

"He was a wonderful man," said Gene Corrigan, who succeeded Krause as Notre Dame's athletic director in 1981, shortly after football coach Gerry Faust had been hired.

"Moose . . . never pretended to be anything other than who he was," Corrigan said. "The thing that will always stick out in my mind was how much he loved his wife and took care of her. Not many people in this world would do what he did. There's so much to be admired. Corrigan came to admire Joyce and Hesburgh, too, for whom he worked seven years.

He had gotten to know Joyce a little bit while Corrigan was serving as Virginia's athletic director, prior to taking the Notre Dame job. But he had never met Hesburgh. His first impression of the university president was a lasting one.

"My first meeting with him came during what constituted my job interview," Corrigan recalled. "Father Hesburgh explained to me that I wouldn't be making reports to the board of trustees, as I had at Virginia. That took me aback, and then he said, 'If I let you report to them, they're going to think you work for them. You work for Ned [Father Joyce] and me. And if you don't do your job, we'll fire you.' He said, 'I don't want you worried about what other people think about your job. How about that?' "

The normally unflappable Corrigan was reverent, moved, and knocked back a bit on his heels all at the same time.

"I mean, this is the first time I ever sat with him," Corrigan continued. "This Notre Dame thing came out of the blue to me. I didn't even know Moose was retiring. They just called me out of the blue to come out and talk to them.

"So Father Hesburgh says to me, 'Do you know all the rules of the NCAA?'

"And I said, 'Father, nobody knows all the rules, but I understand the principle behind them.'

"And Father Hesburgh said, 'That's what I mean. So let me tell you something. If you or any of your people ever violate those rules, you'll be fired. Period. You'll be out of here by midnight.'

"And that's how he was. That's how he would deal with things. Father Joyce shared that same pride about staying within the rules. He would make the point so strong and so carefully that everyone had that same sort of enthusiasm for not breaking the rules."

Hesburgh brought the same kind of passion to everything he did, from serving on the U.S. Commission for Civil Rights during four presidential administrations to heading the college athletic reform movement of the 1990s as the cochairman for the Knight Commission on Intercollegiate Athletics, to reading three books a week for most of his adult life, to playing bridge well and playing golf poorly.

And to simply being a priest.

"From the time I was old enough to think about the future, I wanted to be a priest," said Hesburgh, who turned eighty-seven in May 2004. "And that's all I ever thought about doing. As I grew older, I learned about other careers, but I only wanted to be a priest. And that's all I want to be today.

"When you're a priest, you belong to everybody. You do what you can to help everybody. I didn't aspire to be the university president, but that role allowed me to get jobs in the government, which in turn allowed me to help even more people. But the thing I'm most proud of in my life is simply being a priest."

Hesburgh grew up with that aspiration in Syracuse, New York, the second oldest of five children and the son of a manager of a plate glass company and a housewife. Hesburgh, who speaks six languages adeptly and can read eight, graduated from Gregorian University in Rome. He was ordained in 1943 and received his doctorate from Catholic University in Washington, D.C., two years later.

Shortly, thereafter, he arrived at Notre Dame as a religion teacher. He quickly moved into the Notre Dame administration, becoming executive vice president and chairman in control of the board of athletics. He served in that role for three years before succeeding John J. Cavanaugh as president. At the time, Hesburgh's youngest brother, James, was a sophomore at Notre Dame and was said to have some ambivalent feelings about his brother being president.

Notre Dame was enjoying a national success and acclaim in its sports across the board when Hesburgh and Joyce started their reigns, particularly in football and basketball, the two most visible sports.

Basketball hadn't had a losing season since Walter Halas' squad thirty years earlier, and the Irish would go on to play in their first NCAA tournament that 1952–1953 season. In football, Leahy recovered from a 4–4–1 campaign in 1950 to post back-to-back 7–2–1 marks before breaking through in 1953 with a 9–0–1 mark and a Heisman Trophy for halfback John Lattner. That, however, would be Leahy's last season. Health problems forced him to retire, never to coach again, after the 1953 season.

Hesburgh's and Joyce's first major hire was twenty-five-year-old Terry Brennan, a star halfback for Leahy with limited coaching experience. It showed as the years went on. The two administrators fired the father of four just before Christmas five years later when he refused to resign. Brennan was replaced by Joe Kuharich, who had played for Frank Layden in the late '30s and who came with pro coaching experience.

However, it proved to be another poor fit, as Kuharich and his interim successor, Hugh Devore, combined to go 19–30 over the next five years without a winning season. Basketball moved into a down cycle, too. The team's 9–15

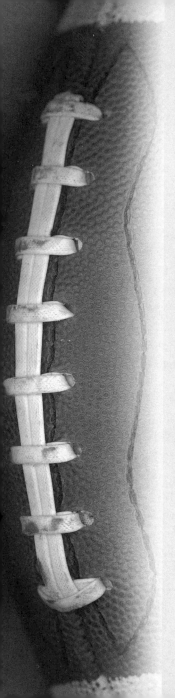

Principle before Politics

The Reverend Theodore M. Hesburgh was never so touched as when a young black man walked into his office in the mid-1950s and handed him a check for $5,000.

"He was one of our first black football players, and he had just been given $5,000 for joining the pros," recalled Hesburgh, president of the University of Notre Dame from 1952 to 1987. "He gave me the check and said, 'Give it to some poor kid, because I was poor when I came here, and you had to buy me a sport coat. Well, now I'm graduating. I can earn my own money. I want to give something back to this wonderful place.'"

Black students had been on the campus for less than a decade at that time, and there were still very few of them. By the 1960s, the numbers began to increase. So did Hesburgh's involvement in the civil rights movement. He had been appointed to the U.S. Commission on Civil Rights in 1957 by President Dwight D. Eisenhower.

"The hypocrisy of segregation in the North is as bad as the rigidity of segregation in the South," Hesburgh said in a 1964 interview with the *South Bend Tribune*'s Jack Colwell. "And if I had to choose, I think I'd choose the South as the better, because at least they're honest about their feelings."

Hesburgh knew he'd rankle some feelings as he pushed for equal opportunities on his own campus.

"It wasn't easy," he said. "When I came here to teach in 1945, there was only one black student on campus, and he was here through the Navy. It was a hundred-year tradition. It had been that way forever. And the myth was that if we let more black students in, in larger numbers, then the white students would leave. We had a lot of kids from southern states.

"Well, there was only one student who I can remember who actually did leave. His mother was upset there was a black student in his dorm, Farley, for which I was a rector. She said, 'Either he's out by tomorrow morning, or my son is back on the train to New Orleans.'

"I said, 'We'll miss your son.'"

Eventually, Hesburgh was missed by the civil rights movement. In 1971, he released a report critical of Richard Nixon's presidential administration and was quickly purged.

"The report said the worst provider of rights for minorities ought to be the best, namely the government," Hesburgh said. "But they indeed had the worst record for hiring minorities in a city that was more than half minorities. Well, that made them look awfully bad."

Hesburgh was asked to hold the report until after the election, but he refused.

"I got the ax," he said.

And wielding the ax, according to Hesburgh, were Chief of Staff H. R. Haldeman, Assistant for Domestic Affairs John Ehrlichman, and Attorney General John Mitchell. Two years later, the three were implicated and eventually imprisoned for their roles in the Watergate scandal.

showing in 1955–1956 was its first losing season in more than thirty years. It was followed shortly after by another losing season in 1958–1959 and then the first back-to-back sub-.500 campaigns (1960–1961 and 1961–1962) since just before Keogan began his stellar twenty-year run in 1923–1924.

Hesburgh and Joyce were sharply criticized and accused of de-emphasizing athletics, this even after they hired Ara Parseghian to replace interim coach Devore in football. Parseghian was well thought of in coaching circles, but some Irish fans couldn't get past his deceptive 36–35–1 record in eight years at Northwestern.

Many blamed academic standards for Notre Dame's fall from football's top echelon, a familiar refrain that resurfaced at the end of both the Gerry Faust (1985) and Bob Davie (2001) football eras. Some Notre Dame followers felt the structure of having two priests run everything at the university, including athletics, had become an outdated arrangement.

Hesburgh, in particular, came under fire for being too spread out in his duties—traveling when he supposedly should have been sitting in his office, and too focused on his passion for boosting the civil rights movement and his other outside ventures.

The clamoring began to subside when plans were unveiled to build the Athletic and Convocation Center and when Parseghian started visiting dorms on campus prior to the magical turnaround 1964 season, giving the students a firsthand look at just what a dynamic leader they were getting.

"I'd have to say hiring Ara was one of the smartest things we did," Hesburgh said. "But Ned's ideal of athletics' place in the academic model and mine had never wavered.

People might have just thought it did. We always believed athletics was subsidiary to academics."

Ironically, as Parseghian dramatically directed the program back to the pinnacle of college football, Hesburgh and Joyce were soon being accused of putting too much emphasis on winning, just as they had during the later stages of the Leahy era.

"We never apologized for winning," Hesburgh said. "We wanted to be the best at everything. We had some great coaches and we had a few who weren't that great, but we survived them and somehow the world went on. The other fellows who weren't spectacular were still good people. That's important."

It was Joyce's duty to keep Notre Dame's image pristine, even when its football bottom line suffered, and he took great pride in the school's largely spotless record with the NCAA.

"Father Joyce was a rock," Valdiserri said. "And not just for Notre Dame. People credit him with saving scholarship athletics in college as we know it, because there was a great deal of push for non-aid sports. He got up in the NCAA convention and made a speech that changed minds and saved the status quo.

"Back here, he was so dedicated and protective of Notre Dame athletics. If there was trouble brewing, he would smell it and put an end to it before it could take shape. You would never dare do anything that would embarrass Notre Dame athletics when he was in office, because you just had so much respect for him."

Joyce was as adept in business as he was in legislating morality. The Honduras native and Spartanburg, South Carolina, product was a certified public accountant for the

The Reverend Edmund P. Joyce (right) meets with Richard and Pat Nixon during a 1956 Nixon campaign stop in South Bend. (Courtesy South Bend Tribune)

first eight years after he graduated from Notre Dame in 1937. He carried that with him when he was ordained as a Holy Cross priest on June 8, 1949, and moved into the Notre Dame administration three years later.

"As the years went on, I don't think Ned had one bad financial year," Hesburgh said. "One year he told us we were underwater a little bit, but I think he was just trying to scare us."

Joyce himself never seemed to be scared about anything, much less the sprawling growth the university underwent between 1952 and 1987 in terms of budget, buildings, and philosophy. When Hesburgh presented Joyce with his first operating budget to balance, it was roughly $9.7 million. Upon their retirement it was $176.6 million. The university's endowment had swelled from $9 million to $350 million over that same period. The research funding went from $750,000 to $15 million. Student enrollment nearly doubled, to 9,600. And women were admitted as undergraduates in 1972. Joyce and Krause launched the first women's athletic programs two years later.

Joyce was also a visionary, especially when it came to the way athletics and dollars related to one another. As early as 1955, he was publicly chafing at the NCAA control of televised football games, an ideal that decades later led to Notre Dame's withdrawing from the College Football Association and signing an exclusive contract to have NBC televise its home games.

Joyce also researched and wrote about how college athletes generally evolved into solid citizens—not because of their physical skills, but because of the lessons they learned in sports.

Joyce and Hesburgh learned those lessons right along with them, including deciphering when it's time to step out of the spotlight. They decided to do it together, retiring on June 1, 1987.

The two then toured the continental United States and Alaska over the next year in a mobile home, logging some 16,000 miles.

"Neither of us had ever been in one of those," Hesburgh laughed. "And what was more challenging, here we were both seventy years old, and neither of us knew how to cook or do laundry or all that stuff, but we survived it."

They then survived a 2,500-mile trip down the Amazon, then a tour around the world aboard the *Queen Elizabeth II*, then a cruise from the southern tip of South America to the Antarctic.

"When we got back, we worked on a number of things together and took vacations together and looked back together," Hesburgh said.

They both had retirement offices issued to them on the thirteenth floor of the library that bears Hesburgh's name and features the noted mural known as Touchdown Jesus. Now just Hesburgh spends his days there, but his thoughts are never far from Joyce, and the memories of their collaborations still inspire him.

Father Joyce passed away on May 2, 2004. He was eighty-seven. "Of course, he always was good with numbers," Hesburgh said. "But most importantly, he was a good person, a true gentleman, and a true friend."

The *Real* Return to Glory

Parseghian's 1964 Team

The same drive almost a year earlier had spooked Ara Parseghian. This time it seemed every porch light was on. Every face that saw the bus rolling from the South Bend airport toward the Notre Dame campus seemed to have an approving glow. The ride itself seemed to be all right turns and green lights.

In the moments ahead, a field house full of admiring students and fans would cheer till their throats hurt, almost taking the sting out of a last-minute upset loss at USC suffered the previous day.

"Oh God, it was magic," recalled Tom Pagna, an assistant coach on that 1964 Notre Dame football team whose storybook run had prompted the impromptu pep rally. "I never saw anything like it in my life."

The same could be said of the 1964 season itself. Under new head coach Parseghian, the '64 Irish did more than just push aside the darkest era in Notre Dame football history—five straight nonwinning seasons, including a 2–7 mark in 1963. They dispelled the notions that the football schedule had gotten too tough, that maybe high academics and championship football had become divergent principles, that the rest of the college football world finally had caught up to Notre Dame—for good.

Even in the aftermath of the 20–17 setback to the rival Trojans that jarred the Irish from their number one perch, perhaps the most profound message Parseghian, the 1964 Notre Dame team, and its 9–1 record sent to those celebrating in the field house that late November evening and all those who wished they could have been there was this: This is only the beginning.

Over the next ten years, Parseghian would coach the Irish to a top fifteen finish in all of them and eight more times coax Notre Dame into the top ten. National titles came in 1966 and 1973. Forty first-team All-Americans were anointed. The richest tradition in sports got a second wind.

Running back Nick Eddy (47) was a central figure in Notre Dame's 1964 resurgence. *(Courtesy* South Bend Tribune*)*

Then, just as dramatically as he had arrived, Parseghian, after the 1974 season, abruptly walked away from coaching forever. A 13–11 upset of number two Alabama and coach Paul "Bear" Bryant in the Orange Bowl punctuated his exit.

"I just got to thinking that here I am supposed to be a sensible person," Parseghian said, "and I'm taking two pills a day for blood pressure. That's not my nature. So I figured I better get out while I still had my senses."

He was fifty-one years old, roughly the same age as the man who succeeded him, Dan Devine, and the man who almost got the job in the first place back in December 1963.

Parseghian had heard the rumors in the days leading up to his mid-December hiring at Notre Dame. The Reverend Edmund P. Joyce, Notre Dame's executive vice president and iron-hand leader when it came to athletics, was supposedly infatuated with the then-Missouri coach. Parseghian read that Devine, however, was entangled by his contract, but Parseghian never pressed the issue with the Notre Dame leadership to see if it was any more than printed innuendo.

After all, a Rochester, New York, newspaper even had legendary NFL coach Vince Lombardi taking the job.

Parseghian had called Joyce a few weeks earlier to find out if Notre Dame was going to make a coaching change. Hugh Devore was the Irish head coach during the 1963 season, but he wore an "interim" label in front of that title the entire time.

Joe Kuharich, 17–23 in four seasons (1959–1962) and not a record above .500 in any of them, defected five weeks before spring practice in 1963 to take a job as the NFL's supervisor of officials. (Kuharich quickly bailed out of that job to resume coaching in the pros.) Joyce then elevated Devore, the Irish freshman coach during the Kuharich regime, to the interim head coaching job. The Irish then backslid from their 5–5 season in 1962 to a 2–7 mark in '63.

"I picked up the phone and asked Father Joyce if they were contemplating a change," Parseghian recalled. "If he was, I'd like to throw my hat in the ring. And if he wasn't and wanted to continue on with Huey Devore, disregard the phone call."

Joyce didn't disregard the phone call. He would later proclaim publicly that one of the reasons Devore wasn't retained was because of his age (fifty-three), a statement that could certainly engender a lawsuit today.

Devore, however, turned out to be an unsung hero in Notre Dame's real return to glory. He was given the title of assistant athletic director, a position without much responsibility or teeth to it. Devore nevertheless worked with Parseghian during the transition, giving the new coach recruiting contacts and information on returning personnel. His attitude in helping Notre Dame was infectious rather than toxic.

Even during his interim season, the second such time Devore had filled that role in his coaching career at Notre Dame, he was a positive force.

Kuharich, a Notre Dame and South Bend product whose freshman coach when he was an Irish player was none other than Devore, had gutted morale during his return to South Bend. He came back to Notre Dame from the NFL and ran the Irish like a pro team. He was distant, aloof, and hardly open to new ideas and directions. Above all, he was convinced that the Frank Leahy dynasty days (1941–1953) were not only impossible to re-create but unapproachable as well.

"This insatiable appetite to win has become so strong, it is ludicrous," Kuharich said often during his four seasons as Irish head coach. The media guides—called "dope books" during the era—were almost laughable in their content concerning Kuharich. His bios read like a litany of excuses why the Irish wouldn't be among the nation's elite teams in a given year.

Interestingly, Kuharich recruited every one of the starters on the 1964 turnaround team. Many of them, like eventual All-America linebacker Jim Lynch, came for the education rather than the football. Lynch picked Notre Dame over Parseghian's Northwestern team and Navy.

"I was probably the only Irish Catholic kid growing up in the Midwest that gets offered a scholarship to Notre Dame, takes it, and his parents are disappointed," Lynch said with a laugh. "They wanted me to go to the Naval Academy, where my older brother went. At any rate, my choice had nothing to do with the personalities of the coaches who were there or anything else. It had to do with the reputation of the school."

Others, like running back Nick Eddy, came to Notre Dame because of connections. Neither Kuharich nor any of his staff saw any film of Eddy. They simply took a recommendation from his Tracy, California, high school coach at face value.

"I didn't even realize Notre Dame was in Indiana," Eddy said. "I thought everything was in California, because that's the only place I ever lived."

How ever they got there or why they came, Devore took them all under his wing. It was an age in which freshmen were ineligible, so Devore spent the freshman practices working on fundamentals. Even the quarterbacks hit the blocking sleds.

"He was like a father figure to us when we were freshmen," said Mike Wadsworth, an Irish lineman and a 1966 grad who went on to be Notre Dame's athletic director a couple of decades later. "And when Huey was the head coach, he brought the Notre Dame spirit back. The 1963 season was such a grim year. The president [John F. Kennedy] was assassinated and all that business. But you have to look at everything in its fullness. And Huey gained our respect for doing the best he could in a very difficult situation."

Devore had gone 7–2–1 in his first interim stint back in 1945. He was the second of two replacements who filled in for Frank Leahy (Ed McKeever coached in 1944) when Leahy was in the Navy during World War II.

Devore then left Notre Dame in 1946 to take the St. Bonaventure head coaching job. The former All-America end bounced around in the collegiate and pro ranks before landing back at Notre Dame. Among his coaching stops was the University of Dayton, where in 1954 his .500 Flyers upset Miami of Ohio, 20–12. It was the only loss in the final two years at Miami for a man named Ara Parseghian and one of only six setbacks Parseghian suffered against thirty-nine wins and a tie in five years at his first head coaching job.

The timing of Kuharich's departure, though, put Devore in a tougher situation than he had ever encountered. He had to throw together a makeshift coaching staff, for one. And he wasn't the most organized guy in the world to start with. But he was resilient.

"The one thing you always knew about Huey was his love for Notre Dame," said Eddy, a running back who blossomed under Parseghian. "What we all learned was how much he loved Notre Dame. As a result, you grew to love it as much as he did. He had a little boy who had cerebral palsy, and he would bring him to practice every once in a while and we'd give three cheers for the little boy. Just seeing him in that setting gave you even more of an appreciation of the type of man he was. It couldn't help but rub off on you and become something you carried in your own life."

Indeed, after a successful run in pro football and a couple of decades working in the insurance industry, Eddy started over as a teacher. A special education teacher.

Parseghian was touched by Devore as well.

Coach Ara Parseghian (center) chats with offensive backfield players (from left) Nick Eddy, Bill Wolski, Larry Conjar, and Bill Zloch during a practice session in November 1965. *(Courtesy* South Bend Tribune*)*

"He could have been very bitter if he wanted to be," Parseghian said. "He was anything but, and I really appreciated every bit of his help."

Parseghian moved so seamlessly into head coaching, it appeared he didn't need much help. But he has a long list of people who touched him along the way and who helped encourage and shape his genius.

It started with his high school coach in Akron, Ohio— Doc Wargo—and continued with Paul Brown when

Parseghian was in the service at the Great Lakes Naval Training Center. Sid Gilman, Parseghian's football coach at Miami, where Ara was a three-sport participant, was another contributor. Then it was back to Brown in the pros followed by exposure to the fiery Woody Hayes, his boss for just a year at Miami.

From a purely X's and O's standpoint, though, Blanton Collier, a backfield coach for the Navy's Great Lakes team, was the man whose brain Parseghian picked most often.

"He was a master technician, a wonderful person, a guy who could express himself," Parseghian recalled. "He was a guy you wanted to play for, because he was always trying to improve you, and he was always doing it in that low-key manner. Even though he was an offensive coach, he had a great defensive philosophy. I felt I was deficient on the defensive side of the ball, so I spent a lot of time with him.

"Each of those guys gave me certain things. But when I talked at clinics. I'd tell them, 'You know, you can't be somebody else. You may admire and take away the good things, but you must always be yourself and not try to be that person. Once you have your own set of fundamental philosophies, then you express them through your own personality. Otherwise, you're going to be revealed as something you're not.' "

Hayes's departure to Ohio State after the 1950 season meant Parseghian was elevated to the head coaching job after just one year as an assistant. To this day he wonders, had he been an assistant longer, if his head coaching career would have lasted longer; that maybe he would have learned to process the adversity better if he could have learned that lesson peripherally as an assistant instead of on the front lines for so many years.

There wasn't much adversity to process at Miami, though. But from there, it was on to Northwestern, which hadn't had a winning record in the four seasons that preceded Parseghian (or in twenty-eight of the thirty that followed him).

It was there that the seeds of the 1964 Notre Dame run were actually sown. After a 4–4–1 campaign in 1956, the Wildcats lost all nine games the following year. Eventually, long after he had left Northwestern, Parseghian came to the conclusion that being the only private school in a league (Big Ten) dominated by state schools had severe disadvantages, but he would hear none of that in 1957. Instead, he grew introspective, dissecting everything from recruiting practices to the equipment the Wildcats used.

"Some of the problems were inherited," Parseghian said. "We paid the penalties for that. But we weren't going to have excuses. One of the great lessons you learn in athletics is that you're going to get knocked down. Every day is not going to be a bright, sunshiny day. You get your tail kicked, but then you have to evaluate why it happened. Just because you get knocked down doesn't mean you're going to stay down."

In his last four years at Northwestern, Parseghian was reunited with Pagna, a star running back for him at Miami who hailed from Parseghian's hometown of Akron.

Pagna had gone on to the pros to play, done a hitch in the military, and started coaching at North High School in Akron when he saw that Parseghian had an opening on his staff going into the 1960 season. But when Pagna went to interview for it, he was taken aback.

"He seemed kind of distant and removed," Pagna said. "And I was a little bit hurt. I always thought we had such great rapport."

That might be an understatement. Severe health problems and the death of his father gave Pagna just one season of high school football. His dream was to go to Notre Dame for college, but he resigned himself to the notion that any college was out of the question. The family had lost just about everything during his father's decline. He needed to work to put food on the table.

Enter Parseghian, who recruited the Akron area for

Miami. He saw Pagna playing in an industrial league basketball game and took him out for ice cream afterward. In just that brief brush, Parseghian recognized both the talent and the heartache that burned inside Pagna. So he helped Pagna get a job at the Goodyear plant. Pagna worked there for nine months, then enrolled at Miami.

While at Miami, Parseghian would hand down his old clothes to Pagna. When Pagna tore a muscle his senior year, Parseghian sent him to the best doctor he knew—the Cleveland Browns' team physician. He even let Pagna and his bride use his home for their honeymoon because Pagna couldn't afford one.

So it was understandable why Pagna left Evanston, Illinois, stung, with serious thoughts of heading to law school or, more realistically, back to the Goodyear plant.

"Later on Ara explained [it] to me," Pagna said. "He said, 'Tom, I was on shaky ground with Stu Holcomb [the athletic director at Northwestern], and I didn't want to bring you into a situation where the next year we're all fired. But you seemed so intent on it, I thought, what the hell, hire him.' "

The chemistry was perfect. Pagna wasn't the only one, but he in so many ways embodied the assistants whom Parseghian was able to attract over the years. Competent. Innovative. Loyal almost to a fault. Pagna, for instance, turned down coaching offers regularly to stay with Parseghian.

He was one of three assistants who made the move with Parseghian at the end of the 1963 season to South Bend. Paul Shoults and Doc Urich were the others. Both Shoults and Pagna stayed for all eleven Parseghian years at Notre Dame.

"I'm not sure my assistants got the credit they deserved," Parseghian said. "But without them, it would have been a different story. Tom, for example, was a people person. He could identify with the players. He just had a natural instinct for the game and the people he was dealing with."

As did Parseghian. He was familiar with Notre Dame's personnel, having played the Irish four straight years (1959–1962), with Northwestern beating the Kuharich-coached Irish all four times.

"When we were at Northwestern, we really admired Notre Dame's talent," Pagna said. "And when we got there, we couldn't believe their talent. It was so much better in terms of depth and size and speed from what we had. At Northwestern, we might have maybe seven, eight good players starting for us. At Notre Dame, they had players that good sitting two deep on the bench. But things were in such disarray.

"A lot of guys on Huey Devore's staff had spent the previous year kind of backstabbing him, because he was the interim guy and they all wanted to be the head coach. We thought, if we can just get organized, we can win at least five games. So we started looking at film, started evaluating our talent, size, and speed."

The real magic performed by Parseghian and his staff came the spring before the 1964 season, when he unearthed talents like senior quarterback John Huarte, who had been rotting on the bench since his arrival from California, and moved many other players to new positions.

Parseghian, for example, slimmed down fullback Jack Snow and made him an All-America wide receiver. Paul Costa and Pete Duranko moved out of the offensive backfield over to the defensive line.

"We had the feeling that he knew what he was doing," Eddy said of Parseghian moves. "The impression that he

Pagna's Detoured Dream

Tom Pagna still considers himself a guy who lived happily ever after, even if it took a while to get there.

Pagna was the offensive collaborator with former Notre Dame head coach Ara Parseghian during all eleven years of Parseghian's brilliant coaching run at Notre Dame. Their history went back much further, though, back to when Pagna was a teenager. And they remain the best of friends today.

That's why it was so painful for Parseghian when he resigned after the 1974 season and neither Pagna nor any of Parseghian's other assistants got so much as an interview for the vacancy. The job went instead to Dan Devine, whom Notre Dame executive vice president the Reverend Edmund P. Joyce had always been fond of and who reportedly had been in the mix eleven years earlier.

"I felt bad about the decision and that I didn't do more," Parseghian said. "I probably had eleven or twelve pages on legal pads when I went to Father Joyce about what my intentions were. I thought I should be replaced by a staff member. Nobody was more disappointed than I was. Tom was well-qualified as far as I was concerned. I would have loved to have seen him get the job, but the one thing I couldn't do was make the selection. That was in somebody else's hands. All I did was try to influence that decision, but unfortunately, I didn't get it done."

Pagna admitted the snub broke his heart. But he picked himself up and eventually landed in the pro ranks as an assistant with the Kansas City Chiefs. He also was the long-time color voice of Notre Dame football radio broadcasts until he was mysteriously replaced during the Bob Davie era.

Pagna's head coaching aspirations were never about ego. They were about sharing his knowledge and passion for the game. They were about touching lives beyond football. And to that end, Pagna didn't need a change in title to do that.

"I can honestly tell you Tom Pagna had more to do with my success than any [other] one person," Notre Dame All-America running back Nick Eddy said. "He was like a surrogate father to me—my dad was never really there for me growing up—and he kind of

Former Irish offensive assistant Tom Pagna takes charge at a practice session during the 1973 season. *(Courtesy Joe Raymond)*

took his place and advised me a lot. For example, it was a conversation with him that eventually convinced me to marry my wife.

"As far as football was concerned, he taught me so much. I had a lot of natural instincts, but he channeled them all in the right direction. I know the chips never fell in the right alignment to get that head coaching job he wanted so much, and I know his heart and soul was with Notre Dame. But Tom did so much good during his time there and beyond. He doesn't have to look back and be disappointed about anything. He can look back and be proud."

gave was that he was always under control, and I think he always gave the impression he was ready to go out and play himself if he could. As a result, you would run through walls for him."

Wisconsin, the 1964 season-opening opponent, seemed to present a rather formidable wall itself. The Badgers had beaten Notre Dame each of the two previous seasons, and having to start the season on the road only added to the mental hurdles.

Early in the game, Snow got behind the Badger defense and let a strike from Huarte slip through his rain-soaked hands. But the two heated up from there, with Huarte throwing for 270 yards and two long TD strikes to Snow, as the Irish thundered past a stunned Wisconsin team, 31–7.

"I always placed a hell of an emphasis on the first game of the year, every year," Parseghian said. "We didn't know how good we were going to be, because we had been going against ourselves. But the attitude had been great, and I felt pretty good about that. It was so important to get that first win. I was basically selling our way and what sacrifices the players had to make to be a good football team. If you want your team to buy into that, you better win right away."

In twenty-four years of coaching, Parseghian lost just one season opener. That was the 0–9 season at Northwestern in 1957.

The upset of the Badgers sent the Irish into the AP top ten for the first time since October 28, 1961, when Parseghian's Wildcats knocked off the Irish 12–10 and sent them into a nosedive.

The '64 Irish followed their conquest of Wisconsin with a rout of another Big Ten team, a 34–15 triumph over

Purdue. Lopsided victories over Air Force, UCLA, Stanford, and Navy vaulted Notre Dame into the number one spot in the polls for the first time in twelve years and stirred Heisman Trophy talk for Huarte, who won the award later that season.

"Ara really did do a good job of keeping us focused," said Jim Lynch, a linebacker who would go on to captain the 1966 national championship team and earn All-America honors that year. "The biggest team you had to worry about beating you was your own team, Ara would say. And so there was always an inner focus about being the best you can be, individually and collectively.

"We knew Ara and the coaching staff were good. I just didn't know how good until years later, after I had been around other coaches and staffs and other methods. He was way ahead of his time, and it took me a while to appreciate just how good we had it."

Notre Dame preserved its number one ranking in its first defense of it, but just barely. The Irish edged Pittsburgh, 17–15, on the road, snuffing a Panther drive at the 17 yard line. The Irish then routed Michigan State and Iowa to set up a showdown at USC in the season finale. The four-game sweep of the Big Ten was astounding, given Notre Dame's collective 3–17 record against its Midwest neighbors over the five previous seasons. That included an 0–5 mark against Michigan State.

The Irish still were under their self-imposed bowl ban, so a victory over the Trojans on November 28 would mean a national title. USC rallied, though, late, pushing across the winning score with 1:33 left to end the magical run. Notre Dame finished third in the AP poll behind Alabama and Arkansas.

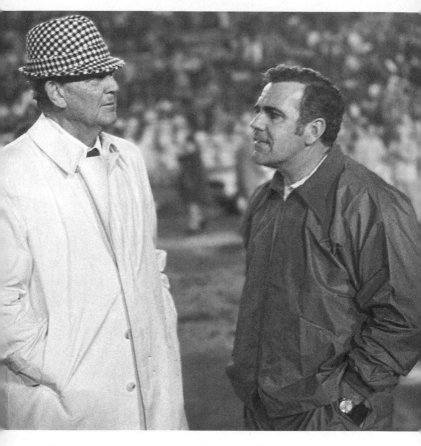

Alabama coaching legend Paul "Bear" Bryant (left) chats with Notre Dame coach Ara Parseghian at the 1973 Sugar Bowl in New Orleans. Parseghian and the Irish defeated Number 1 Alabama, 24–23, on December 31 to win the national championship. (Courtesy Joe Raymond)

It often took Parseghian four days to get over a loss, but the cheering throng in the field house that last Sunday in November almost made the hurt go away.

Parseghian would go on to reinvent himself several

times over the next decade. He would move into new realms of political endorsements and side businesses. He would raise huge amounts of money for multiple sclerosis and later Niemann-Pick Type C Disease. He would help rescind Notre Dame's bowl ban. He would beat Devine's Missouri team 20–7 in 1970 in the only meeting between Parseghian and his eventual successor.

And then he would walk away for good.

"Oh, I'd get the itch to come back to coaching once in a while," said Parseghian, whose postcoaching pursuits included being a college football analyst and color commentator for television. "I'd find myself doodling defenses and offenses, and then an opportunity with a pro team would come up, but I'd push it away every time. I think I did the right thing."

He certainly lived up to the name his father had given him. Ara was a king in Armenian legend who symbolized new life. And that he gave to the Notre Dame football program.

Yet it came so close to never happening. Had Northwestern athletic director Stu Holcomb not been so meddling, Parseghian may never have picked up the phone to call Father Joyce.

Even after Parseghian had agreed to be the Irish coach, there were "thirty hours of indecision," as the *South Bend Tribune* called it. Parseghian did not sign his contract right away, and there was speculation that he never would.

"If you knew why I did that, it's safe to say you wouldn't think any less of me or Father Joyce," said Parseghian, who has dodged the question deftly for four decades.

"He walked out of the press conference, and it could have been a dozen things, nobody really knows," Pagna said. "But he did tell me one day, as he came down Notre Dame Avenue toward the Golden Dome, he got this eerie feeling."

It was the same drive he would take a year later after the USC loss.

"He said, 'Tom, I was born and raised Catholic, but I never really practiced it,'" Pagna related. "He said, 'I married a Protestant girl, and I guess I question whether I have the right, with all the heritage and with all the tradition and everything. Do I have the right to coach here?' He took that seriously, you know.

"And, of course, I'm Roman Catholic, and I told him, 'Ara, hell yes you have the right. You know you can bring to this school more than they ever dreamed.'

"And that he did."

The Legacy of Lou

Giving Back

T ony Rice never really had much of a hankering to get to the bottom of why Notre Dame and Lou Holtz parted ways on the evening of November 30, 1996. Maybe it was because he was too deep in shock.

"I guess part of you thinks he was going to be there forever," said Rice, the starting quarterback on Notre Dame's 1988 national championship team under Holtz.

Maybe it's because Holtz's relationship with his players *is* forever.

The former Notre Dame head football coach was there for Rice when the South Carolina native got snagged by a new NCAA admissions rule called Proposition 48 back in the fall of 1986. He was there the next year when Rice finally was able to get into a game and lined up behind the offensive guard on his very first collegiate play.

Holtz was also there in 1989 when some bigoted Irish followers suddenly threw race into the conversation when Rice, Notre Dame's first black starting quarterback, couldn't replicate another title run—even though the Irish lost just one game that season and routed top-ranked Colorado, 21–6, in the Orange Bowl.

But most significantly, as far as Rice is concerned, Holtz was there when Rice had to take the back roads to a professional football career, when that dream ultimately crumbled, and when Rice labored to find his niche in the business world once football ended for good.

"He has never let me down," Rice said of Holtz. "He's done a lot as far as opening doors for me, getting contacts for me. As a football player, Coach Holtz prepared me for the real world. And when the real world gets too real, he's still there for me."

That, indeed, is the most enduring part of Holtz's legacy at Notre Dame.

Yes, he did give the Irish more traditional and tangible contributions. His 100 wins in eleven seasons (1986–1996) is the highest victory total amassed at the school other than Knute Rockne's 105. Holtz produced a national title and came tantalizingly close on two other occasions (1989 and 1993).

He pulled Notre Dame football out of one of the program's deepest funks—the Gerry Faust era. And he did it while playing roughly 40 percent of his games against top twenty-five teams. (Holtz's Irish squads were a collective 32–20–2 against ranked teams during his run.) With his dynamic team and personality, Holtz made Notre Dame football an attractive enough commodity for NBC to invest millions in televising the school's football games.

But what Rice and other Irish players of that era remember most was that Holtz was always about the bigger picture—life. And he never let time, distance, or circumstance distort that.

"There isn't anything more important in this world than helping people," Holtz reflected.

Holtz was not without his flaws and challenges. He never seemed far removed from a full-blown crisis or a persistent rumor that he was entertaining a job offer. He went through assistant coaches, at times, like worn underwear.

In his later years—after the athletic director (Gene Corrigan), president (the Reverend Theodore M.

Hesburgh), and executive vice president (the Reverend Edmund P. Joyce) who hired him were long gone—Holtz clashed with the Notre Dame admissions office over what constituted a good risk. He was frustrated that he was criticized by his own administration for what they perceived as alarming attrition when Holtz felt that he was simply purging toxic players for the good of the program.

Bob Davie, Holtz's defensive coordinator for his last three seasons in South Bend and eventually his successor as head coach, even questioned Holtz's sanity to seemingly everyone with an office in the Joyce Center but Holtz.

But what was never debatable was Holtz's love for the school. He loved it when he was in parochial grade school and his classes were dismissed using a recording of the Notre Dame Victory March. He loved Notre Dame enough to have an escape clause put in his coaching contract at the University of Minnesota in the mid–'80s. And he still plans to be buried at Notre Dame...when the time is right.

"It's only appropriate," he said, "because the alums buried me every Saturday."

No one ever beat Holtz to the punch line, especially when the target was himself.

"I'm 5'10", 152 pounds," Holtz proclaimed at his Notre Dame introductory press conference on November 27, 1985. "I wear glasses, speak with a lisp, and have a physique that makes me look like I've been inflicted with beriberi and scurvy for most of my life. I was 234th out of a class of 278 coming out of high school. I couldn't get into Notre Dame. I couldn't ever get into St. Vincent's of Latrobe [Pennsylvania]. I went to a state institution [Kent State], because they had to take me.

"And here I am the head coach at Notre Dame."

Former Irish coach Lou Holtz (left) and quarterback Tony Rice (9) share a light moment on the sidelines during Notre Dame's national title run in 1988. (Courtesy Joe Raymond)

Some observers, including *Sports Illustrated*, thought Holtz was committing career suicide. Sure, he had been a fixer-upper at several of his previous coaching stops, but many thought Faust's failures were due more to the changing college football landscape and Notre Dame's unwillingness to adapt to it than the former high school coaching phenom's shortcomings as a college coach.

Corrigan had come aboard as Notre Dame's athletic director in 1981, shortly after Faust was hired. And it was clear early in Faust's tenure that a mistake had been made and that it wasn't going to get any better by itself. Corrigan just wasn't sure what options he had.

"I remember after Gerry's third year, I got a call from somebody at the *Chicago Tribune*, who asked me about Gerry's contract and the length of it," Corrigan said. "And I kind of beat around the bush with the reporter. The next day I got a call from Father Hesburgh, who very seldom got directly involved in athletics. He called and said that he had read the article in the paper. He said, 'You're kind of struggling with this Faust thing, aren't you?'

"And I said, 'Yeah, because Gerry is struggling. It's a difficult time.'" Corrigan continued. "I wasn't sure that Gerry was going to be able to make it. Kids were unhappy and talking to the press about transferring. You know how those things go."

"And Father Hesburgh said to me, 'Well, how long *does* he have on his contract?'

"And I said, 'Two years.'

"He said, 'Unless he dies, he'll be here two years. Period.'"

Faust announced his resignation on November 26, 1985, four days before Notre Dame's 1985 season finale against Miami, and finished with a five-year mark of 30–26–1. He moved on to coach at the University of Akron, where he put together a 43–53–3 mark in nine years. Prior to taking the Notre Dame job, Faust's eighteen-year record at Cincinnati Moeller High School had been a Rockne-like 174–17–2, including seven unbeaten seasons, five Ohio state titles, and four mythical national championships.

Holtz might not have been available to follow Faust had Ohio State not mishandled their courtship of him following Woody Hayes's firing at the end of the 1978 season. The Buckeyes ended up hiring Iowa State coach Earle Bruce instead.

Holtz, like Bruce, came out of the Hayes lineage. They were both assistants on the 1968 Ohio State national championship team, but Holtz—then the head coach at Arkansas—was the higher-profile candidate. He also had made a seamless transition at Arkansas in following a legend, Frank Broyles.

The fact is, according to Holtz, had then–Ohio State athletic director Hugh Hindman offered Holtz the job instead of asking him to interview for it, Holtz might still be wearing scarlet and gray now. He surely would have been in 1979.

"I coached there, they knew me, they knew what I was all about," Holtz said. "But if it was an interviewing process, I was not interested. They said it was an interviewing process with five other guys. I said, 'I'm sorry, I can't do that.'"

Bruce, though, was more than willing.

"I was forty-nine years old," Bruce said. "I had been at Iowa State six years. If I was going to be Ohio State's head coach, it was going to have to be at that time. Because of my age, there wasn't going to be enough time to get it the next time. So it was either take it then or wonder what could have been. I knew they wanted Lou Holtz, and when that didn't happen, I called the athletic director to tell him I was interested."

Notre Dame's hiring process with Holtz was much more streamlined.

Faust informed Corrigan of his decision to resign at 10:45 on the morning of November 26. The Notre Dame athletic director immediately went into a meeting with Father Joyce and by 4:00 P.M. had permission from Minnesota athletic director Paul Giel to speak with Holtz.

"I knew Lou had an out clause in his contract, because I had talked to him previously about it," Corrigan said. "We were able to move fast, because we had had conversations."

Joyce, meanwhile, gave Corrigan carte blanche to hire whomever he wanted and appoint whomever he wanted to a search committee. Corrigan decided on a search committee of one: former Notre Dame coach Ara Parseghian.

"Ara was my sounding board," Corrigan said. "Of course, I kept Father Joyce and everyone else who needed to be apprised of what was going on. But between Ara and I, we thought Lou would be most suitable.

"I had known Lou when he was at William & Mary and at North Carolina State. I knew all about him. I knew he was a guy who was kind of like Ara. I'm a history major, so I studied the people who had succeeded as coaches at Notre Dame. And the common thread was that they all pretty much were guys who had succeeded as college head coaches at other places before they got to Notre Dame."

Holtz was even successful at Minnesota, a moribund program when he arrived in one of the strangest coaching moves in college football history. He took a team that was

1–10 the year before his arrival and had essentially quit on coach Joe Salem and was a competitive 4–7 in his first year and 6–5 and bowl bound in his second. Attendance ballooned from 20,000 per game to 50,000 in two years.

Holtz was offered the Notre Dame job late in the day that it opened up. He publicly declared the need to sleep on the decision, though many thought that was simply a ploy to soothe Minnesota fans who already felt jilted.

Irish fans, meanwhile, were ecstatic.

"My only real piece of advice I gave him," Corrigan said, "was, 'Don't stay longer than eight years.' I said that because it is such a high-pressure job. Ara told me he probably should have left a year or so before he did. He said it got to him, and that he didn't realize how much until after he stepped away. He said, 'If I had stayed on and coached Notre Dame much longer, I'm not sure I'd be alive today.' It really does take a chunk out of you."

Holtz, forty-eight years old at the time of his hiring, didn't follow Corrigan's advice or really his own. He pledged a wide-open offense devoid of the option plays that had made him successful at Minnesota as well as some of his other previous coaching stops.

"We want to play offensive football with as little risk as possible," Holtz said in the month following his hiring. "Option football is high-risk offense."

Holtz backed that thought up by recruiting pure drop-back passer Kent Graham for the incoming 1987 freshman class, but Rice—an option type in Holtz's first class—beat freshman Graham out in 1987. Graham subsequently transferred to Ohio State. Option remained, at the very least, a partial staple in Holtz's offenses in the post-Rice years, with the exception of the 1993 season.

Like many of Notre Dame's great coaches before him, Holtz won a national title with someone else's seniors, namely Faust's. He also coached a Heisman Trophy winner, Tim Brown, in 1987, who was a Faust recruit, yet gradually but noticeably Holtz put his imprint on the recruiting classes.

Speed became a premium. He recruited defensive backs to play linebacker, linebackers to play defensive line, and defensive linemen to play offensive line. Like Parseghian, he liked to move players around. Unlike Parseghian but much like Rockne, Holtz liked to take chances on kids.

Rice and John Foley, members of his first recruiting class, were two such players. Rice was a 6', 197-pound quarterback from Woodruff, South Carolina, and Foley, a 6' 3", 230-pound linebacker from Chicago. Both were prep All-Americans with a tedious list of college suitors, though Faust's Irish coaching staff had not been pursuing Rice.

And both got snagged in the NCAA's controversial Proposition 48 rule. Maybe the most divisive rule in college sports history, Prop 48 was passed in 1983, but Rice's and Foley's 1986 freshman class was the first to be affected by it. Prospective student-athletes at that time were required to achieve both a 2.0 grade-point average in a core curriculum and a 700 or better score on the SAT.

High school counselors, students, and parents alike were often confused by the rule, including just what constituted core classes and what didn't. Notre Dame was even caught off-guard. After admitting Rice, Foley, and basketball player Keith Robinson, the school never again took a student-athlete who did not meet Prop 48 guidelines. Yet none of the three were ever academically ineligible, just their SAT scores, and all three graduated in four years.

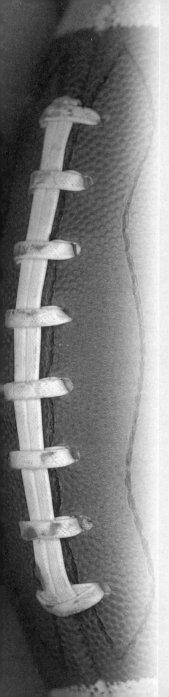

Lou Looks Back

As Notre Dame moved into the Bob Davie era (1997–2001), Lou Holtz's persistent silence on his exodus only prompted the unanswered question to grow louder:

Did he jump, or was he pushed?

Holtz puts the blame squarely on his own shoulders.

"You reach a point in your life where you say, 'This is pretty good. We've achieved an awful lot. Let's just keep it here,'" he said. "It was the dumbest thing I've ever done. I wasn't tired of coaching, I was tired of maintaining.

"What I should have done was set dreams and goals and ambitions for this university and the football program that nobody thought were possible. As long as you have a dream, you have a million thoughts and ideas, and you have enthusiasm and excitement. When you try to maintain something, you lose your enthusiasm and any originality. You never have a reason to celebrate."

Holtz landed at South Carolina after a two-year sabbatical of sorts. He actually openly flirted with the Notre Dame job when Davie was fired in December 2001, but maintains he was simply helping the search process along, not asking for it to end with him.

He has never stopped being a fan, though.

Former Irish coach Lou Holtz makes a point to his team during practice at Notre Dame Stadium in the fall of 1988.
(Courtesy South Bend Tribune)

For Rice and Foley, Proposition 48 meant they had to stay completely away from athletics for a year—no practices, no games, no spring football. The stigma that came along with being a Prop 48 casualty was far less forgiving.

"People frowned on us and looked down on us," Foley recalled. "You'd be walking to class and you'd hear, 'Pfft, there goes a Prop 48. He doesn't belong here.'"

"The one incident that really sticks out in my mind," Rice said, "was a pep rally before the first game of my freshman year. I was sitting there feeling bad already that I wouldn't be playing, and this guy gets in my face and tells me how dumb I am, because I couldn't pass my SAT.

"I felt as bad as could be, but as the years passed, I proved him wrong."

Actually, many Proposition 48 nonqualifiers did. The same year Foley and Rice matriculated to Notre Dame, eleven Prop 48s headed to universities in the neighboring Big Ten. Like Rice and Foley, none of them were ever academically ineligible. And nine of those eleven graduated.

"I laugh at those people now who made that rule," said Foley, who after graduation listened to motivational tapes in the car, metabolized every word, and eschewed the corporate ladder for a high-speed elevator. "I don't want to sound arrogant, but I probably make two to three times what the president does. But then again, I owe it all to Notre Dame and to Lou Holtz."

It wasn't always a love fest. When Rice and Foley became eligible in 1987, they saw Holtz's sharp, demanding edge. It was even more so that fall, with Notre Dame coming off a 5–6 season that seemed to encourage everyone but Holtz himself.

"The assistants kind of had to take me aside and tell me

Coach Holtz wasn't mad at me," Rice said. "They said, 'Listen to the words and not the tone. He doesn't hate you. He's just trying to make you better.' So I took that into consideration."

Foley had a harder time with it. Called the best linebacker prospect to come out of Chicago in fifteen years by recruiting analyst Tom Lemming, Foley struggled, in part due to injury, until he moved to the defensive line late in the 1987 season. He later admitted he actually grew to hate Holtz that season, loathed his methods, and was confused about what he stood for.

Then came the hit, and he no longer had to wonder what Holtz was about. It came during the Cotton Bowl at the end of the 1987 season, roughly eight months before Notre Dame would start its national title run.

Foley was a terror on special teams that New Year's Day, even as Texas A&M was pummeling the Irish 35–10. But on Texas A&M's third kickoff of the day, the Aggies sent two players after Foley—"one to distract me, one to take me out," he remembers.

"I got hit so hard, I couldn't think straight," Foley said. "I mean, one guy put his helmet in my neck. I played the rest of the game, but my career was over. I lost the use of my right arm for about a year. The doctors told me that it might get better for a while but that down the line it would affect me tremendously. Eventually, they said, the pain would come back and it might never go away."

That wasn't the scariest part for Foley, however. Being separated from football forever was.

"I honestly had a lot of emotional problems when I got hurt," Foley said. "I actually, no exaggeration, thought my life was going to end. I didn't think I was smart enough to

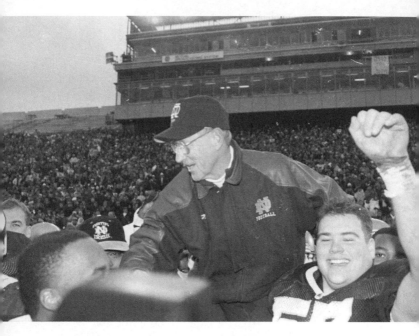

Lou Holtz gets a ride off the field from his players following his final home game as Notre Dame's head football coach. The Irish defeated Rutgers 62–0 on November 23, 1996 at Notre Dame Stadium.
(*Courtesy Joe Raymond*)

get a real job. I never had confidence that I could do anything out in the real world."

Rice got past Holtz's tempering tactics and led the Irish to an undefeated season that fall. Foley's 1988 experience was just as magical, if not more.

"I wasn't taking school very seriously when I was playing ball," Foley said. "And I really didn't think Lou Holtz cared about grades anyway. Well, let me tell you something, Lou Holtz cares as much as anybody. Lou Holtz spent more time with me after football was no longer there for me than when I was a player. The whole university supported me. I owe everything to Notre Dame."

Foley's doctors were right. The pain came back when Foley was twenty-seven years old. His spine swelled. His whole body ached. Even now, the pain sometimes gets so severe, it wakes him out of a dead sleep. Yet Foley never thinks of what might have been in football and he never asks, "Why me?"

"I feel like the luckiest guy in the world," he said. "I live with a lot of pain, but I've been given a lot of gifts. The best thing that ever happened to me was for my football career to end. It opened the door to my dreams."

And the man who held the door open, Foley said, was Holtz.

Irish Traditions

A Rich But Murky Heritage

For a school that takes such great pride in the precision of its football records, its heritage, and its history, it is fascinating that the origins of so many of Notre Dame's traditions read like a multiple-choice test. Such notable staples as the Fighting Irish nickname and the Notre Dame Victory March have disputed beginnings, but their place in Irish lore is undeniable.

Another undeniable fact is that you don't mess with tradition.

A case in point was coach Tyrone Willingham's first Irish football team in 2002. The team had gotten off to an 8–0 start and had climbed into the top five of the national polls when rival Boston College came to town.

You could almost hear a collective groan when the Notre Dame team emerged from the stadium tunnel decked in green jerseys rather than its traditional blue.

Green jerseys had been the norm during some earlier eras of Notre Dame football and had been used upon occasion all the way back to Knute Rockne's time (1918–1930). But they took on a negative vibe during the Gerry Faust era (1981–1985), even though the embattled coach won two games with them.

Boston College upset Willingham's Irish, 14–7, at Notre Dame Stadium on that November 2 afternoon. And to this day, some of the sharpest criticism aimed at Willingham has been about the wearing of the green.

Willingham claimed the move was orchestrated as a show of unity with the fans, who had been wearing green all season, rather than the Faustian purposes of firing up this team.

Actually, the jerseys did fire up the team—the *other* team.

"I think it excited us," Boston College coach Tom O'Brien answered when asked about Notre Dame's fashion statement. "Our guys took it as a great sign of respect that we made it, that we were somebody to be reckoned with. Just that [Notre Dame] needed the green jerseys to beat us."

Heading into the 2004 season, the losing streak in green jerseys had reached three games.

A positive postscript to the story was that a running back prospect named Travis Thomas was in the stadium the day Notre Dame lost to Boston College, and he loved the green jerseys. He committed to the Irish shortly thereafter.

Touchdown Jesus

It wasn't supposed to have anything to do with football, but the image itself and the proximity to Notre Dame Stadium has made Touchdown Jesus a favorite among Irish football fans.

The 132-foot-high stone mosaic on the south side of Hesburgh Library faces the stadium. Before the stadium was expanded for the 1997 season, Touchdown Jesus could be easily seen from most seats. Now it is largely obscured.

The Hesburgh Library itself was built on the site of historic Cartier Field, on which Knute Rockne's teams played, and opened its doors on September 18, 1963, as the Memorial Library, at the start of Notre Dame's 122nd

Touchdown Jesus, which sits just north of Notre Dame Stadium, wasn't intended to be part of Irish football lore, but has become so anyway. (Courtesy Joe Raymond)

academic year. In 1987, it was renamed for President Emeritus Theodore M. Hesburgh. The fourteen-story library holds more than two million volumes and can accommodate half of the student body at any one time.

The mosaic depicts Jesus Christ surrounded by the world's great saints and scholars. With the image of Christ's upraised arms looming high over the north end zone of the football stadium, the mosaic became Touchdown Jesus. The landmark became so famous that even a book has been written about it.

Touchdown Jesus is one of three campus landmarks that unintentionally took on football themes. The others are We're Number 1 Moses and Fair Catch Corby.

The Moses statue, made of bronze and located just west of the Hesburgh Library, depicts Moses with his flowing robes at the foot of Mount Sinai, chastising the Israelites who have fallen into idolatry. He is pointing to the heavens as if to declare there is but one God.

Fair Catch Corby sits in front of Corby Hall. It depicts Chaplain William J. Corby with his arm raised in the act of giving general absolution to the Irish brigade before it went into action in the Battle of Gettysburg. Corby also served two separate stints as Notre Dame's president (1866–1872, 1887–1891).

The Leprechaun

Maybe Clashmore Mike just ran out of good luck or maybe it was simply coincidence, but the terrier mascot that had been part of Notre Dame football for roughly three decades faded quietly into history in the mid-1960s.

The Leprechaun replaced the dog early in the regime of Ara Parseghian, with the Leprechaun eventually being registered as an official university trademark in 1965. The Irish football team won the national championship the next year.

Clashmore Mike's last prominent appearance as Notre Dame's mascot came on the cover of the 1963 *Notre Dame Football Dope Book*. Interim football coach Hugh Devore is seen kneeling with the dog in the cover photo and holding its leash. Captain Bob Lehmann also appears on the cover, but seems oblivious to the terrier, even though it is only inches away. The Irish suffered through a 2–7 season that year.

The terrier is one of those Notre Dame traditions whose origins are somewhat disputed. The Irish media guide claims the first terrier was named Brick Top Shuan-Rhu and was presented to coach Knute Rockne the week of the Notre Dame–Pennsylvania football game in 1930. Another account says the first dog was named Tipperary Terrance.

In any event, most of the subsequent terriers, including one given to coach Elmer Layden in 1935, went by Clashmore Mike. He was the subject of a book in 1949 called *Mascot Mike of Notre Dame*. The dog had a column in the game-day programs in the 1930s and '40s. It even claimed to have preferences for other mascots, with its nemesis being Navy's goat.

With the growth of Notre Dame's overall sports programs, the school now uses two Leprechauns a year. There is an intense one-day tryout each year, which includes demonstrating the ability to perform a traditional Irish jig, having to perform a motivational speech, and participating in a mock pep rally. Each Leprechaun is fitted

The leprechaun mascot has been a Notre Dame staple for the past four decades. (Courtesy Joe Raymond)

with a unique tailor-made uniform that he gets to keep at the end of his reign.

The Leprechaun and its familiar logo constitute one of Notre Dame's eighteen registered trademarks. And the school is quite serious about the trademark.

In 1995, the *South Bend Tribune* ran an image of the Leprechaun pointing to the left. A representative from the school's licensing department promptly sent a letter stating that the mascot should *only* be portrayed pointing to the right.

Around the same time, Notre Dame was recruiting a standout center prospect for basketball named Jason Collier. Collier attended Central Catholic High School in Springfield, Ohio, a town settled by Irish immigrants.

Not surprisingly, the school adopted the nickname Fighting Irish, but it also painted the Notre Dame leprechaun mascot on the gym floor. Soon after the Irish coaches visited the gym to scout Collier, a letter from Notre Dame's general counsel landed on the desk of Ann P. Colliflower, then the director of development at Central Catholic.

Central Catholic was asked to remove the logo, which it did at a cost of thousands of dollars. A new leprechaun, this one with its arms folded over its chest, replaced the Notre Dame version, putting up its dukes. The high school promptly registered *its* new trademark.

Oh, and Collier? He spurned Notre Dame for Indiana.

The Notre Dame Victory March

It is the most recognizable song in all of college sports and one of the most popular of all American songs. Even before Northern Illinois University librarian William Studwell proclaimed the Notre Dame Victory March as the number one college fight song in 1990, there was little doubt about it. The song, created in 1908, became so popular over the years that by 1964, 29 percent of the nation's elementary and secondary schools had school songs based on the Victory March.

In most accounts, brothers Michael Shea and the Reverend John Shea, both Notre Dame graduates, were inspired to write a school song after attending Notre Dame football games during the 1908 season at Indiana and Michigan.

"I wonder," John was reported to have told his brother, "if we couldn't work up a pep song that belonged to Notre Dame."

"I've got a tune running through my head," Michael fired back. "I'll see you in a few days, and we'll go to work on it."

And what they came up with still stands today:

Cheer, cheer for old Notre Dame,
Wake up the echoes cheering her name,
Send a volley cheer on high,
Shake down the thunder from the sky.

What though the odds be great or small,
Old Notre Dame will win overall,
While her loyal sons are marching,
Onward to Victory.

In Murray Sperber's book *Shake Down the Thunder*, he points out the discrepancies as to just when the inspiration crystallized into the classic it has become. One story has the Shea brothers visiting campus as alumni in 1908 and meeting at a reading room in Sorin Hall, where Michael pounded out the melody on the piano over and over. John then fit words to the music as they went along. Another version had Michael and John collaborating at their family's home in Holyoke, Massachusetts, after John had returned from the seminary.

There is also conflicting evidence as to just how much of the creative genius was supplied by each brother, but Michael definitely wrote the music, and John at least had a hand in the lyrics.

In a *South Bend Tribune* account of the story, the two brothers returned to Sorin Hall the next day to polish the final project, but this time the reading room was occupied. So they walked over to the nearby Sacred Heart Church and finished the job on the church's organ.

John Shea recalled the first public performance of the song taking place Easter Sunday of 1909 in the rotunda of the administration building. The Notre Dame football team's rise under Jesse Harper and their propensity to play away games on big stages helped further popularize the song to a national audience. It was even reported that during World War I, American soldiers found the Victory March something they liked to march to. The song first appeared under Notre Dame copyright in 1928.

Michael went on to be a pastor of St. Augustine's in Ossining, New York, until his death in 1940 (the Notre Dame media guide incorrectly reports his passing as happening in 1938). John, who lettered in baseball at Notre Dame, went on to become a state senator in Massachusetts and lived in his old hometown of Holyoke until his death in 1965.

The Fighting Irish

At the height of the Miami–Notre Dame football rivalry in the late 1980s, an entrepreneurial Notre Dame student came up with an idea for T-shirts to celebrate the rivalry, which featured the phrase "Catholics vs. Convicts."

Had Notre Dame stuck with its original nickname, the Catholics, it could have charged the student its standard 8 percent royalty fee, but at some point, perhaps as early as 1889, Notre Dame's sports teams switched over to their current moniker, the Fighting Irish.

What is known for sure is that university president the Reverend Matthew Walsh officially adopted the Fighting Irish nickname in 1927 and that for most of the 1800s, Notre Dame's sports teams were known as the Catholics.

In between there was a long list of nicknames—the Warriors, the Hoosiers, the Benders, the Domers, the Catholic Collegians of Indiana, the Nomads, the Ramblers, the Papists, and the Horrible Hibernarians.

Like many college nicknames, it is possible an act of derision gave birth to the Fighting Irish nickname. The Notre Dame media guide suggests that one version of the story had Notre Dame leading Northwestern at halftime 5–0 in a football game at Evanston, Illinois, in 1899. The Northwestern fans supposedly began to chant "Kill the Fighting Irish. Kill the Fighting Irish."

However, Notre Dame didn't play Northwestern on the road in 1899. The teams did meet in Evanston in 1889, so it's possible the roots were in that 9–0 Notre Dame victory in the only game the school played that season.

Another version had Notre Dame trailing Michigan in a 1909 matchup when a member of the team reportedly yelled at his ethnic Irish teammates, "What's the matter with you guys? You're all Irish, and you're not fighting worth a lick." Notre Dame came back to win the game, 11–3, and the *Detroit Free Press* did make a reference to the Fighting Irish in its accounts of the game. However, five years earlier, the *Milwaukee Journal* made a Fighting Irish reference of its own.

A footnote to that 1909 Michigan game: fullback Pete Vaughan scored the go-ahead touchdown with such force that he reportedly broke a goalpost. Legend had it that Vaughan did the damage with his head, but years later Vaughan said it must have been his shoulder that hit the goalpost.

The version of how the team got its nickname that the university seems to endorse—whether the nickname came from derision or inspiration—is that Fighting Irish embodies a "never say die spirit" and "Irish qualities of grit, determination, and tenacity."

Gold Helmets

Yellow, not gold, and blue were Notre Dame's official colors when the school was founded in 1842. Yellow was said to symbolize the light and blue the truth. However, sometime after the dome and statue of Mary atop the main building were gilded, gold and blue became the official colors of the university.

The unadorned gold helmet has been in style since Ara Parseghian's first season, in 1964. There were slight variations in the seasons leading up to that.

Under interim coach Hugh Devore in 1963, the Irish gold helmets featured big white uniform numbers on the

Painting the Notre Dame football helmets with gold paint and real gold dust before games is a long-standing tradition. (Courtesy Joe Raymond)

side. In the Joe Kuhariche era (1959–1962), they featured a big green shamrock.

The current helmets feature actual gold dust in the paint and mimic the school's famed golden dome. Managers mix gold dust bought from the O'Brien Paint Company with lacquer and lacquer thinner. The helmets are painted on Friday nights before home games and Thursday nights when the team is traveling.

Sign of the Times

Most of the Notre Dame players who touch the gold placard with blue letters as they head up the stairs from the locker room to the Notre Dame Stadium tunnel assume the sign has been there for decades, if not eons.

PLAY LIKE A CHAMPION TODAY, the sign reads.

Few at the university know its exact origins, but its popularity took off in the '90s when NBC began televising Irish football games on a regular basis and sometimes showed the players tapping the sign before spilling out onto the field.

The sign actually first appeared outside the Notre Dame locker room during the Dan Devine era (1975–1980), even though many of Devine's own former players assumed it was the work of Devine's predecessor, Ara Parseghian.

"No, it wasn't me, though I like the sign a lot," Parseghian said with a chuckle. Coincidentally, Parseghian's son-in-law, James Humbert, is involved in making replica signs and souvenirs to sell to Irish fans.

The Navy Rivalry

It is the oldest intersectional rivalry in the country and also the most lopsided. Navy and Notre Dame have met every year in football since 1927 and will do so for the foreseeable future.

The reason is simple: gratitude.

During World War II, Notre Dame was in financial trouble and might have closed were it not for some programs the Navy instituted at the school. Legendary coach Frank Leahy and 1947 Heisman Trophy winner John Lujack were big Navy fans as well, having both served in that branch of the service during the 1944 and 1945 football seasons.

Sometimes Navy may ask itself if Notre Dame is really doing it a favor. Heading into the 2004 season, the Irish had won forty meetings in a row—an NCAA record for most consecutive wins against one opponent in college football history.

The Irish Guard and Notre Dame Band

Their job description includes leading the Notre Dame band, performing Irish jigs, cheering on the sidelines, and protecting the band, but during one game of Tyrone Willingham's first season as Notre Dame football coach in 2002, the Irish Guard had a little trouble with a few of those duties. During a 31–7 rout of Willingham's old school, Stanford, on October 5, 2002, the Irish Guard was caught napping—literally.

The NBC cameras showed several of the guard's members asleep during the game. The university promptly suspended the ten-man, kilt-wearing squad for a game.

For most of its existence, though, the Irish Guard has helped wake up the echoes at Notre Dame home football games. Established in 1949 by then–band director H. Lee Hope, the guard originally played the bagpipes.

That ended after about five years, when the group evolved into its current version of precision marchers with stoic expressions. All guard members are required to be 6'2" or taller and have been since 1949.

In 2000, Molly Kinder crossed the gender barrier and became the first female member of the guard. The 6'3" Kinder, who graduated in 2001, played on a state championship basketball team her senior year at Holy Angels Academy in Buffalo, New York. She also was a member of the Irish rowing team for a year and a half.

The Notre Dame band itself has a much longer history than the Irish Guard. In fact, it has been around for roughly a century longer and predated the inception of the Irish football team by some four decades. The band did play at Notre Dame's first-ever football game — in 1887 against Michigan.

The band's origins go back to at least 1846, when it was referenced that the band played at graduation. Some historians, however, believe it might have been around since 1842, the year Notre Dame was founded. In either case, the Notre Dame band is the oldest college band in continuous existence in the United States.

University founder the Reverend Edward Sorin was professed to have been a clarinet player, as was former longtime athletic director Moose Krause. Legendary coach Knute Rockne played flute for Notre Dame.

Before the band played at football games, its early purpose was to lift the spirits of the Notre Dame student body. It also honored those students over the years who served their country in the military by playing in the university's main circle as students left for battle all the way back to the Civil War.

The late Robert O'Brien, who died in the summer of 2003, had a significant influence on the band. He was the director from 1952 to 1986 and had a hand in many band traditions, including the singing of "America the Beautiful" and the reciting of the preamble of the Constitution during football pregame performances, as well as the design for the distinctive plaid sash worn by Notre Dame band members today.

He also wrote "The Victory Clog," a jig the Irish Guard performs after every Notre Dame touchdown.

After the Cheering Stops

Life after Football

They have all settled comfortably into their nine-to-five lives, with no regrets, no gnawing feelings of what might have been.

Ron Powlus, the most recognizable name among the foursome, is the only one of those former contemporary Notre Dame quarterbacks who is more than vaguely familiar with the other three: Blair Kiel, Jake Kelchner, and Zak Kustok.

Kiel is the only one of them who played a down in the NFL, though all four dabbled in professional football. Three of them endured a head coaching change while at Notre Dame. Two of them transferred. One was expelled.

But what binds them together to this day is the courage they showed when adversity pushed them to the limits of what they could handle—and perhaps a bit beyond. Another common, if not more significant, thread is the Notre Dame spirit they all tapped into and still carry with them today.

You can see it in Kelchner's smile when he holds his infant son in his arms. You can see it in Kiel's eyes every summer, when he hosts a charity golf tournament that raises roughly $50,000 annually for Crohn's Disease, a sometimes

Ron Powlus (center) prepares to throw as Randy Kinder (25) upends a Purdue lineman during Notre Dame's 35–28 victory over Purdue on September 9, 1995. (Courtesy Joe Raymond)

debilitating illness of the gastrointestinal tract. You can hear it in the lilt in Kustok's voice when he talks about going back to his old high school and helping out with the football team. And you can sense it in every one of the many charities Powlus lends his name to these days.

"I realize I have a name in the area," said Powlus, who has never lost the air of celebrity in his hometown of Berwick, Pennsylvania, which just happens to be the place where he and his family decided to start life after football. He doesn't run from the spotlight these days, but he doesn't seek it either. Sometimes, though, it still seeks him.

Which is why he was the honorary chairman of two different heart walks, roughly three months apart, in the summer of 2003, why he is involved in fund-raising for Alzheimer's Disease, why he anchored a cancer telethon in northeastern Pennsylvania recently.

"Life is good," decreed Powlus, who has been working in a home loan center for Washington Mutual Bank since the late summer of 2003.

His bank career carries considerably less scrutiny than his football life once did. Notre Dame had never recruited a player who was so celebrated, so dissected, so plumbed with other people's expectations, and the Irish may never again.

"I didn't look at the attention as a negative at all," said Powlus, now thirty, married, and the father of a toddler. "It was just part of life. I don't have any problems with anything I went through. It's just the way it was."

What most people didn't know during Powlus's Notre Dame career (1993–1997) was the private hell he lived during the 1996 season, his third as a starter and final season under Lou Holtz. During that season, Powlus's mother, Susan, was diagnosed with congestive heart failure.

"That's when we first started dealing with it as a family," Powlus said. "But she dealt with it and is doing OK now. She has taken control of her life in a good way. So when the heart disease people came to me for help, I was more than happy to. In fact, I'm happy to help out in any way I can. Even though my college football career didn't work out the way some people think it should have, I was given a lot, and for that, I'm grateful. And the best way to show your gratitude is to give back."

As a high school kid in Berwick, Powlus lived a storybook existence. He was so far ahead of the curve at his position, he felt the attention but never the pressure. It came that easily to him. During Powlus's senior season (1992), Berwick went 15–0 and was USA Today's national high school football champion. He was dubbed the nation's top prospect by Parade magazine, USA Today, Gatorade Circle of Champions, SuperPrep magazine, and almost every recruiting service. Yet Powlus and those around him never let the wooing process get out of hand.

"I know for a lot of these kids [recruiting] really is a crazy process," he said. "But for me, it wasn't as crazy as it was enjoyable. One of the main reasons was that early on, to be very honest, I realized I was in demand. I was going to have the choice of where I wanted to go. And I think because of that, it gave me a little more control of the situation."

So Powlus's high school coach, George Curry, and his father, Ron Sr., shut down the recruiting process during the younger Powlus's high school football senior season.

"I talked to recruiters during the summer, but the only contact they could have with me after that was letters until the season was over," Powlus said. "Once the season was over, I really got into it. I wasn't burned out, because it never dragged on. It wasn't overwhelming. It was fun. It was nice to be wanted."

Powlus, his father, Coach Curry, and a teammate took a tour of twelve schools the spring before Powlus's senior season.

"That was a great idea," he said. "A recruiting weekend can be so manufactured. But when you go in the spring, we saw coaches coaching for real. We saw players playing hard. It wasn't a setup. And Notre Dame came out of that process on top. The question became, can anyone top Notre Dame? That was the measuring stick."

Powlus narrowed his field to four and took visits to those schools: Miami, Penn State, Pittsburgh, and Notre Dame.

"The thing that helped me make the decision—and I tell this to kids all the time now—is prioritizing," Powlus said. "You have to make a list of what's important to you. Do you want to play close to home? Do you want to be far from home? Is playing time important?

"You also have to be honest with yourself about how really good you are and how you fit in. And the final thing is, football is going to end someday. You have to ask yourself, 'Is this the school I want to graduate from?' When I did all those things, the choice to go to Notre Dame was easy."

The tough part for Powlus came after he got to Notre Dame. On the fifth play of the final preseason scrimmage his freshman season (1993), Powlus suffered a broken clavicle. "I think that day I was going to be named the starter," he said.

Instead, Powlus missed the season (he reinjured the clavicle in practice on October 17), but had a spectacular debut the next season, throwing for 291 yards and a school record-tying four touchdowns in a 42–15 rout of Northwestern in the 1994 season opener.

Then came the curse. TV analyst Beano Cook proclaimed Powlus would win two Heismans after witnessing the Northwestern game. Powlus didn't come close to winning one, and because of that, because the highlight of his short pro career was a nice one-year run in

NFL Europe, very few people even remember that he finished his collegiate career well ahead of the Joe Montanas and Joe Theismanns of the world on top of Notre Dame's career passing yardage list.

"It's unfortunate the expectations that are placed on kids even before they ever step on the field," Powlus said. "For me, it wasn't so much the recruiting rankings, it was the two Heisman thing. So in most people's eyes, I never lived up to expectations.

"In fact, I went through a lot of things at Notre Dame, and my parents and friends thought it was terrible. At the same time, that's part of being the quarterback at Notre Dame. That's part of what you're agreeing to by signing that letter of intent. It's unfortunate, but it's part of the deal. You need to be strong and look past the negative things that come with exposure.

"Hey, you can't change the past, and I wouldn't want to. I think it's made me a better person. And the bottom line is, I had a great time at Notre Dame. It still is the place for me."

And perhaps it will be for his young son too.

"He was born on St. Patrick's Day, 2002," Powlus said. "How could he not be a Notre Dame fan?"

Jake Kelchner still is one, even though he never saw the field at Notre Dame and was dismissed from the school after a tumultuous first two years there.

"I had a transition period of growing up, and it just happened to be when I was at Notre Dame," said Kelchner, who turned thirty-four in the summer of 2004 and who lives within 30 miles of Powlus in northeastern Pennsylvania. "I think I tried to go out and enjoy life just a little too much — not having the discipline to stay on the books. But the mistakes I made turned out to be great lessons learned. I

Jake Kelchner, pictured here in action during his senior season at West Virginia, finished with a flourish at WVU after suffering through growing pains at Notre Dame. (Courtesy Dan Friend/WVU Photographic Services)

took those experiences and went on to bigger and better things."

Kelchner played at the same high school as Powlus (Berwick), fashioned an identical 15–0 record as a senior quarterback, and led his team to the Pennsylvania large-school state title as Powlus would four years later. He even broke his collarbone as a freshman, just like Powlus did.

But their Notre Dame experiences were quite different. In fact, Kelchner was all set to go to the University of Pittsburgh, but he reconsidered when he heard rumblings about then-Panthers coach Mike Gottfried's future being on shaky ground. Gottfried indeed was fired in December of Kelchner's freshman season at Notre Dame over a dispute with the Pitt administration.

As highly touted as Kelchner was as a quarterback recruit, the guy who got the Powlus-type publicity in the 1989 recruiting class was fellow QB Rick Mirer. Mirer grew up just forty-five minutes from the Notre Dame campus, in Goshen, Indiana, and was considered the nation's top quarterback prospect.

"I knew Rick was coming and had all the hype," Kelchner said, "but I just thought of it as another one of those challenges you go through. I told myself I had the tools. I'd just go at him. I honestly thought I'd win the job. It didn't bother me where Rick was ranked. I didn't lack confidence."

But what Kelchner lacked was maturity. Mirer saw considerable backup duty as a freshman in 1989 to national championship QB Tony Rice (1988), but the separation between Mirer and Kelchner wasn't perceived to be dramatic. Kelchner did travel with the team as a freshman but was a no-show quite often in the classroom.

By the time he broke his collarbone during the annual Blue–Gold game in the spring of 1990, Kelchner was in a serious academic hole. After a summer in which he took more than a full load trying to play catch-up, Kelchner ended up getting booted by the academic powers-that-be. At Holtz's suggestion, Kelchner enrolled at nearby Holy Cross Junior College.

"It was the whole Rudy thing," he said, referring to Notre Dame's most famous walk-on, Dan "Rudy" Ruettiger, who earned his way into Notre Dame through Holy Cross.

"I never lost touch with the football team, but more importantly I got in touch with the part of me that was responsible. I got my grades up where they needed to be. I was in the best shape of my life. I was throwing the ball like I never had. It was an exciting time. And the best part about it, they honored their word. They were going to let me back into Notre Dame."

The announcement of Kelchner's return was just days away when he went out on a date and his life changed forever in the early hours of the morning of July 25, 1991.

"It's real simple," he said. "I had three or four drinks and was on my way home. A cop pulled me over and said I was swerving. The charge was reduced to reckless driving, but that didn't matter to Notre Dame. I was finished. And the worst part of it was there was no one to blame but me. I was so frustrated, I packed my bags. I was ready to come home and work in the Wise Potato Chip plant. That was it. But Coach Holtz was so great; he wasn't going to let that happen."

Holtz was unsuccessful in getting Notre Dame to reconsider letting Kelchner back in, but he was able to get Kelchner a second chance in football and in college. He asked Kelchner where he would like to go, since Notre Dame was no longer an option. Kelchner's best friend was at West Virginia, and so were two of his former high school teammates.

"Coach Holtz got on the phone right then and there with [then–West Virginia coach] Don Nehlen, and started talking to him," Kelchner said. "He talked me right up, but he was honest with him. He said I had some growing up to do, which I did. But he was great, and I was at West Virginia the next day."

However, Kelchner had to sit out the fall of 1991 due to NCAA transfer rules, marking the third straight year since he had left Berwick in which he did not see game action. An elbow injury truncated Kelchner's season in 1992, though he did play in a handful of games. By the time Kelchner finally got an unimpeded chance to start in the fall of 1993, Powlus's much-anticipated debut was unraveling back at Notre Dame due to his own broken collarbone.

But Kelchner carried the banner for Berwick just fine that fall. And at a school that produced the likes of Major Harris, Mark Bulger, and Jeff Hostetler, among others, Kelchner left WVU as its single-season and career leader in passing efficiency. He also obtained a degree in education.

Still, the NFL showed only mild interest. Kelchner tried to stoke that dream with a four-year stint in the Arena Football League (Tampa, Milwaukee, Florida, Grand Rapids) and a one-year tour of duty in what is now NFL Europe (Barcelona), but having his ribs separated when he was pounded into a wall in Arena League play coaxed him into life after football.

Kelchner settled back in familiar surroundings, hooking up with a cabinetry company in Milton, Pennsylvania. He worked his way up to a management position and married in the summer of 2000. Today, he wouldn't change a thing about his life.

"I have a great wife who I met at West Virginia," he said. "I've got a little girl and a little boy, who are just great to be around. I've got friends and family. I also got to touch my dream finally and to prove to myself how good I could be.

"But I'll never trade those days at Notre Dame for anything. I still follow the team. I still talk to some of my old teammates. And I'll never forget Lou Holtz. I still speak highly of him and the whole staff. What a great experience. What a great place to grow up."

Zak Kustok was a big Holtz fan too, which is largely why he verbally committed in the spring of 1996, just a few weeks after the ink on the previous class's letters of intent had dried. Like Kelchner, though, Kustok never saw the field at Notre Dame and ended up writing his happy ending elsewhere. And when he did, Holtz was watching from a distance.

Holtz was at South Carolina and Kustok at Northwestern when Holtz called Northwestern coach Randy Walker one afternoon and asked him to relate to Kustok how proud he was of the last quarterback Holtz recruited during his eleven-year run at Notre Dame and a player he never got a chance to coach.

"It meant so much to me that he thought I turned into the player he always thought I could be," said Kustok, who was one of five finalists for the Davey O'Brien Award, emblematic as the nation's top quarterback, while a senior at Northwestern. "And my days at Notre Dame also mean something to me.

"Obviously, things didn't work out for me at Notre Dame. But if I had to do it all over again or if I were a senior in high school right now, I'd choose Notre Dame. The reasons I wanted to go to Notre Dame—the tradition, the people, and everything that goes along with being at Notre Dame—I got to experience that, and that's something I wouldn't trade anything for."

What he would trade willingly is the era in which he played. Shortly after Kustok's senior season at Carl Sandburg High in Orland Park, Illinois, came to a close, Holtz announced he was leaving Notre Dame. Kustok had not yet signed his letter of intent, but he chose to honor his commitment to new head coach Bob Davie anyway.

Kustok's freshman season turned out to be a great learning year on and off the field. Powlus was a fifth-year senior starter, but Kustok, as the number three quarterback, got to travel to all the games without burning a year of eligibility. Off the field, Kustok made the dean's list his first semester.

"The best part of that year was being around Ron Powlus," Kustok said. "I thought he was a great quarterback, and I looked up to him. But I looked up to him even more as a person. I watched how he handled all the negative things that were being said about him, the way he just handled it and took it in stride. I think that's the most valuable thing I learned from him, handling the media, handling playing each week, handling the adversity."

Kustok would be getting his own adversity in abundance the following spring after Powlus had exhausted his eligibility. Junior Jarious Jackson moved from backup to front-runner in that spring's quarterback derby. Kustok figured he would move up to number two. But during the second practice of the spring session in 1998, Davie yanked Kustok out of the huddle and told little-used Eric Chappell to go in.

"I couldn't figure out what was going on," Kustok recalled. "Our quarterbacks coach, Mike Sanford, kind of pulled me over and was like, 'I think Coach Davie just wanted to see how you handle adversity.' But I thought it was all kind of weird."

It got weirder. Kustok ended up with a 63 percent completion rate during the spring drills, far better than Chappell and even Jackson. But Davie explained Kustok's slippage on the depth chart as a change in philosophy. The Irish were going to commit to a run-oriented option attack.

Kustok worked on the option on his own all summer long, but when fall drills began, he was never given an opportunity to run it in a scrimmage and rarely in practice. He strayed further and further from any relevance in the quarterback mix. Freshman Arnaz Battle leaped ahead of him. Then, one day, Kustok found himself running the scout team—basically becoming a tackling dummy for the number one Irish defense.

"I asked Coach Davie about it," Kustok said, "and every time he'd say the same thing, 'You're doing a really good job. Just keep up the hard work.' But it didn't mean a thing. I thought I was better than the guys ahead of me, but I wasn't even being given the opportunity to prove it. That's what bothered me the most. So as much as I loved the school and my teammates and everything, I couldn't stay there anymore.

"I had always dreamed of being in the spotlight, being on TV, everything that went along with being at Notre Dame and the reasons I chose it in the first place. I knew those dreams didn't have a chance to be fulfilled with Coach Davie there. My own teammates told me that. I felt

Irish quarterback Zak Kustok scrambles during the team's Blue–Gold intrasquad spring game in April 1997 as linebacker Bobbie Howard (27) closes in. (Courtesy Joe Raymond)

that I'd be cheating myself if I didn't give myself a chance to be the best I could be. I had to try."

Kustok's transfer was a wild ride. He left after Notre Dame's fourth game of the 1998 season and landed at Moraine Valley Community College in Palos Hills, Illinois, roughly 6 miles from where he attended high school. He did not play football there, but the academic calendar allowed Kustok to transfer to a Division I school in the fall of 1999 without sitting out that entire year.

After initially verbally committing to Kansas, Kustok ended up at Northwestern. Then-Wildcats coach Gary Barnett told Kustok that he couldn't take him at first, because he promised a high school prospect, John Navarre, that he wouldn't recruit any other quarterbacks in his class. But Navarre ended up visiting Michigan after he committed to Northwestern, which infuriated Barnett. He then invited Kustok and his father to come up and visit, so he could offer the younger Kustok a scholarship.

As the Kustoks were getting in the car, they heard on the radio that Barnett had resigned to take the job at Colorado. Randy Walker ended up replacing Barnett and offered Kustok a scholarship. Kustok went on to be a starter for two and a half seasons, helped Northwestern tie for the Big Ten championship his junior year, and set school career records for completions (644) and passing yards (7,487).

"It wasn't a matter of vindication," Kustok said. "I wasn't trying to prove my doubters wrong, and there were plenty of them. I wanted to prove to myself I could do it. And for all the people who believed in me and supported me, I wanted to do it for them."

There were a litany of ironies in Kustok's departure, not the least of which was the fact that Kustok, the quarterback who supposedly couldn't run, ended up being North-western's all-time leader in rushing yards by a QB (1,294) and rushing TDs (22) as a quarterback. And the call from Holtz to Walker that long-ago afternoon was not just to compliment Kustok but for Holtz to pick Walker's brain about planned quarterback runs out of the shotgun formation.

Another irony is that late in the 1998 season at Notre Dame, Jackson suffered a serious knee injury trying to take a safety against LSU. Chappell and Battle filled in the next game, and the Irish were upset 10–0 by a Sun Bowl–bound USC team that had just given up thirty-four points the week before to UCLA. The loss knocked the Irish out of the lucra-tive BCS bowl mix and into the second-tier Gator Bowl.

Notre Dame ended up changing its offensive identity the following season to a pass-oriented offense, with Jackson setting a single-season record for passing yardage. Chappell was dismissed in the fall of 1999 for allegedly breaking NCAA rules. He finished his career as a defensive back at Alabama A&M. Battle ended up moving to wide receiver in the spring of 2000.

Davie, meanwhile, was fired in December 2001. One of the persistent problems that led to that decision was a never-ending quarterback quandary, which Davie's successor, Tyrone Willingham, is still trying to rectify. From the start of the Davie era and the signing of Kustok to the end of the 2003 season, nine QBs were recruited to Notre Dame on scholarship. Eight of them ended up either switching schools, switching positions, or both. Starter Brady Quinn is the lone exception. The Irish signed two QB prospects in February 2004, Darrin Bragg and David Wolke.

"I still follow their team all the time," said Kustok, who moved into the business world after tryouts with the NFL's

Miami Dolphins and the Green Bay Packers didn't solidify into anything more than opportunities to try out for other teams. The twenty-five-year-old lives in Chicago and trades federal funds at the Chicago Board of Trade.

"There were difficult times there," Kustok said of Notre Dame, "but the things that stick out in my mind are running out of the tunnel for the Georgia Tech game, my first game, and the first game in the expanded stadium. It was the pep rallies. It was walking from church to the stadium after chapel. It was unbelievable tradition and unbelievable people. I got to experience that, and no one can take it away from me."

Kustok tries to bring a little of that to his volunteer coaching every time he returns to his high school alma mater, Carl Sandburg High.

Blair Kiel gave a lot of thought about getting into coaching himself, but he never went that route—well, not in the traditional sense. Since the winter of 2003, he has been working for Caskey Achievement Strategies, a sort of corporate coaching service for businesses.

"It's great," said the forty-two-year-old Columbus, Indiana, native. "My commitment to my own kids kept me from diving into teaching and coaching, like I always wanted to. I didn't want the travel, and this allows me the best of both worlds."

He also embraces raising two teenagers, an experience that is considerably less stressful than many other stretches in his life, including his four years at Notre Dame (1980–1983). But he is finally at peace with his Irish football experience and is realizing all the good that came out of all the pain.

"It took me a long time to realize everything happens for a reason," said Kiel, who lives in the Indianapolis

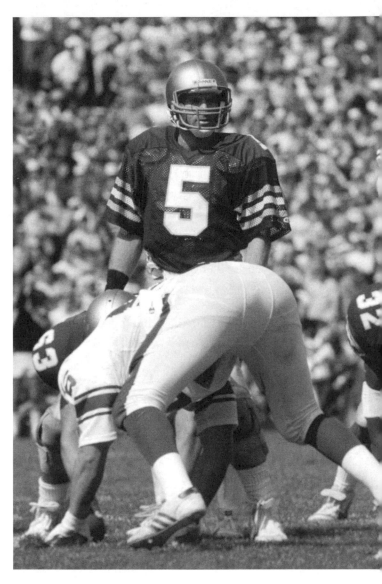

Blair Kiel gets set to take the snap for Notre Dame in this home matchup with Michigan State. (Courtesy Joe Raymond)

suburbs with his son and his daughter. "I also have come to realize I have no control over a lot of those circumstances, and they are teaching me a lot about life."

Kiel's parents, Fritz and Sylvia, were always great teachers of life, too. They provided him opportunities—like installing a set of goalposts in the family's side yard—but they also gave their oldest son room to make his own mistakes and pick himself back up when he did.

But nothing could have prepared any of them for what was to unfold late in Kiel's career at Notre Dame. His high school career at Columbus East mirrored that of Powlus, and so did many of his prep accolades. Ultimately, his college choice came down to Notre Dame and Lee Corso's Indiana Hoosiers, although Tennessee, UCLA, Michigan, and Purdue were all suitors that made it through the initial paring-down process.

Upon verbally committing to the Irish, Kiel proclaimed he wanted to play right away and he wanted to win the Heisman Trophy.

"That's too hilarious," he said. "I'm sure I did say that, but I just don't remember it. If I were coaching somebody, I'd make sure they didn't say something like that. It's good to have lofty goals and everything, but wow, that's funny."

The funny thing was that under Dan Devine, Kiel did become a starter during his freshman season and showed flashes that year that he had Heisman-esque potential. But Devine abruptly retired after the 1980 season, and Notre Dame brought in high school coaching phenomenon Gerry Faust from Cincinnati Moeller.

Kiel never saw the Devine retirement coming and had enough bad vibes from his initial meetings with Faust that he strongly considered transferring.

"I really liked Coach Devine," Kiel said. "He was a quiet guy, but a real neat person. My family and I grew very close to him. So after he announced he was retiring, I was really having trouble dealing with it. Then John Scully, a fifth-year center on the team, came to my room and took me out. He told me, 'You go to a school because of the school, not because of the coach. And Notre Dame is the finest university you'll ever attend.' That talk is what got me to stick it out."

Faust had been critical of Kiel even before showing up at Notre Dame. The criticism continued once he came aboard for the 1981 season. It was written at the time that Faust not only did things to shake Kiel's confidence, but he also blamed his quarterback when his own college coaching inexperience came to light.

"I took the fall," Kiel said. "And most of it was unfair, quite frankly. I was bitter about it for a long time. But then Gerry came out with a book and said he screwed me. He admitted he did not treat me fairly and shouldn't have done some of the things he did to me. If nothing else, it made me feel better about what happened, years later."

At the time, the frustrations continued to build. Kiel considered again transferring at the end of his sophomore season, but he stuck with Notre Dame. By the time he was a senior, the NFL scouts who once figured Kiel was a given for playing on Sundays, now began to wonder if his development had become so arrested during the Faust era that he was now a long shot at best.

Kiel, though, kept his mouth shut until the third game of the 1983 season, a 20–0 loss at Miami. In the rain, Kiel threw a pass to tight end Mark Bavaro on an option route in which Bavaro turned the wrong way.

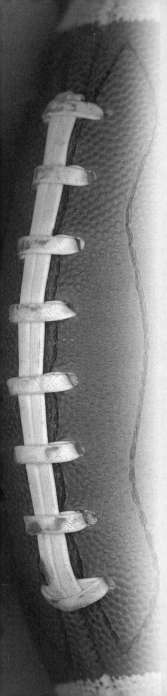

For Starters

Heading into the 2004 season, here's how Notre Dame's quarterbacks since 1975 have fared in their first collegiate starts:

Brady Quinn, freshman;
September 27, 2003
   The bottom line: number 20 Purdue 23, Notre Dame 10
   Stats: 29–59–4, 297 yards, 1 TD; 8 carries for 25 yards
Pat Dillingham, sophomore;
October 5, 2002
   The bottom line: number 9 Notre Dame 31, Stanford 7
   Stats: 14–27–1, 129 yards, 0 TDs; 2 carries for –20 yards
Carlyle Holiday, sophomore;
September 29, 2001
   The bottom line: Texas A&M 24, Notre Dame 3
   Stats: 6–13–2, 73 yards, 0 TDs; 23 yards on 12 carries
Matt LoVecchio, freshman;
October 7, 2000
   The bottom line: number 25 Notre Dame 20, Stanford 14
   Stats: 10–18–0, 100 yards, 2 TDs; 36 yards on 13 carries
Arnaz Battle, junior;
September 2, 2000
   The bottom line: Notre Dame 24, number 23 Texas A&M 10
   Stats: 10–16–0, 133 yards, 2 TDs; 50 yards on 12 carries

Eric Chappell, senior; November 28, 1998

The bottom line: USC 10, number 9 Notre Dame 0

Stats: 0-3-2, 0 yards, 0 TDs; 33 yards on 7 carries

Jarious Jackson, senior; September 5, 1998

The bottom line: number 22 Notre Dame 36, number 5 Michigan 20

Stats: 4-10-1, 96 yards, 2 TDs; 62 yards on 16 carries

Tom Krug, junior; November 18, 1995

The bottom line: number 8 Notre Dame 44, Air Force 14

Stats: 8-13-1, 96 yards, 0 TDs; 13 yards on 3 carries

Ron Powlus, sophomore; September 3, 1994

The bottom line: number 3 Notre Dame 42, Northwestern 15

Stats: 18-24-0, 291 yards, 4 TDs; 6 yards on 2 carries

Kevin McDougal, senior; September 4, 1993

The bottom line: number 7 Notre Dame 27, Northwestern 12

Stats: 6-8-0, 135 yards, 0 TDs; -16 yards on 5 carries

Paul Failla, freshman; September 28, 1991

The bottom line: number 8 Notre Dame 45, Purdue 20

Stats: 1-1-0, 10 yards; 11 yards on 2 carries

Note: Rick Mirer replaced Failla beginning with the second series.

Rick Mirer, sophomore; September 15, 1990

The bottom line: number 1 Notre Dame 28, number 4 Michigan 24

Stats: 14-23-1, 165 yards, 1 TD; 12 yards on 10 carries, 1 TD

Kent Graham, freshman; November 7, 1987

The bottom line: number 9 Notre Dame 32, Boston College 25

Stats: 6-8-1, 111 yards, 0 TDs; 7 yards on 3 carries

Tony Rice, sophomore; October 17, 1987

The bottom line: number 11 Notre Dame 35, Air Force 14

Stats: 1-5-1, 10 yards, 0 TDs; 70 yards on 9 carries, 2 TDs

Terry Andrysiak, sophomore; November 9, 1985

The bottom line: Notre Dame 37, Mississippi 14

Stats: 11-15-1, 137 yards, 1 TD; -7 yards on 2 carries

Scott Grooms, senior; October 13, 1984

The bottom line: Air Force 21, Notre Dame 7

Stats: 12-35-1, 117 yards, 1 TD; -9 yards on 12 carries

Steve Beuerlein, freshman; October 1, 1983

The bottom line: Notre Dame 27, Colorado 3

Stats: 8–12–0, 133 yards, 0 TDs; no rushing attempts

Jim O'Hara, senior; November 20, 1982

The bottom line: Air Force 30, number 18 Notre Dame 17

Stats: 14–23–0, 216 yards, 2 TDs; -21 yards on 3 carries

Blair Kiel, freshman; October 11, 1980

The bottom line: number 7 Notre Dame 32, number 13
Miami (Florida) 14

Stats: 4–17–0, 35 yards, 0 TDs; 28 yards on 11 carries, 1 TD

Tim Koegel, sophomore; September 22, 1979

The bottom line: number 17 Purdue 28, number 5 Notre
Dame 22

Stats: 6–18–1, 81 yards, 1 TD; 0 yards on 4 carries

Rusty Lisch, sophomore; November 20, 1976

The bottom line: number 3 Notre Dame 40, Miami (Florida) 27

Stats: 5–11–0, 102 yards, 1 TD; 9 yards on 15 carries, 3 TDs

Joe Montana, sophomore; October 4, 1975

The bottom line: Michigan State 10, number 8 Notre Dame 3

Stats: 2–5–1, 19 yards, 0 TDs; no rushing attempts

Rick Slager, senior; September 15, 1975

The bottom line: number 9 Notre Dame 17, Boston College 3

Stats: 7–12–0, 72 yards, 0 TDs; no rushing attempts

"Mark came over to me and said, 'I'm sorry, I blew the route,'" Kiel recalled. "At the same time, Gerry was coming out to me and saying that I was the worst quarterback in the history of quarterbacks and that I stunk. He and I actually got into it. I had some choice words for him, and I ended up getting benched four games my senior year."

On came Kiel's roommate on the road and true freshman Steve Beuerlein. But instead of letting their moments together become awkward, Kiel did everything he could to help the first-year Irish player.

"That's one of the things Steve's parents thanked me for afterwards, for handling Steve and helping him the way I did," Kiel said. "I put everything else aside, because I was also captain of the team. That was a bigger responsibility than whether or not I played, and I took it very seriously."

Kiel regained his number one status by sparking a rally in Notre Dame's 1983 regular-season finale, then started and finished in a 19–18 Liberty Bowl victory over a Doug Flutie–led Boston College team.

He went on to the pros as an eleventh-round draft choice of the Tampa Bay Buccaneers. He lasted eight seasons as primarily a backup QB in Tampa, Indianapolis, and Green Bay. He also held for place kicks and punted in the NFL. His proudest moment came in Milwaukee one autumn afternoon in 1990.

Packers starter Don Majkowski went down with an injury, and Kiel nearly rallied Green Bay from a 20–0 deficit. The Packers fell just short in a 20–14 loss. The performance, which came in front of his high school coach, John Stafford, his high school athletic director, Dennis Sylvester, and his brother, Kip, earned Kiel even more playing time down the stretch run of the season. He ended up throwing for a career-high 504 yards while completing 60 percent of his passing attempts that season.

Three years later, he was in the Arena Football League and was taken off the field on a stretcher at Richfield Coliseum near Cleveland on June 19, 1993, when, as the Cincinnati Rockers quarterback, he felt his entire left side go numb after a hit.

"It was a scary time," he said. "I got blindsided by two different guys. I remember saying if I could get up and walk, I was never going to play again."

He broke his promise with himself long enough to hook on with the Canadian Football League's Toronto Argonauts the next season. Kiel quickly realized the fire was gone. At least, he reasoned, he got to touch his dream, for more than a decade.

That was despite a bout with Crohn's Disease in the mid-1980s that almost quelled his pro football career before it could get legs. The ailment came back in the late '90s as well, when football was a memory, but Kiel credits the drug Remicade with helping his life return to normal—or as normal as he could hope for.

Two blood clots that lodged in his lungs four years ago almost killed him. A painful divorce made him even more introspective. A full plate of life limited his opportunities to return to Notre Dame in person for a game, though he did follow the Irish on TV and still does. During the one game he went back for, he just happened to run into someone familiar in the coaches' office. It was none other than Gerry Faust.

"He was very friendly and cordial," Kiel said. "So was I. I don't have any bad feelings toward him anymore. At the time, I sure did. I thought he was affecting my career. But I got to live a dream anyway that most people don't get to. And so for me to hold a grudge against anybody is stupid."

To steer his kids away from football just wasn't going to happen, either. Kiel made sure there were goalposts built in the yard for the next generation.

"My family is always what kept me sane, what kept me grounded through all the tough times, and I want to be that for my kids," he said. "And part of who I am is my Notre Dame experience. So, in that light, I wouldn't do anything over. I have no regrets. Notre Dame was a special place, despite everything I went through. And it will always be."

About the Author

Eric Hansen has been covering college sports since 1983 and has won seven national awards from the Football Writers Association of America over the past decade for his coverage of college football. He was associate sports editor at the *Columbus* (Ind.) *Republic,* and college sports writer and columnist at the *Hammond Times.*

Hansen is currently the managing editor of *Irish Sports Report*, a national Notre Dame sports publication, as well as a staff sports writer for the *South Bend Tribune.* He is a native of Cleveland, Ohio, who grew up in Columbus, Ohio. Hansen resides in South Bend, Indiana, with his sons Antonio and Blake.